Every Insult and Indignity
The Life, Genius and Legacy of
Major Patrick Ferguson

What people are saying about
Every Insult and Indignity

Every Insult and Indignity is an intriguing study of Major Patrick Ferguson's famed breechloading rifle and a fine example of what experimental archaeology can achieve. The authors, Bryan Brown and Ricky Roberts, are well-respected members of the Revolutionary War living history community who together have more than sixty years of experience in the hobby. They have produced a much needed and welcomed treatise.

---- Anthony J. Scotti, Jr., Ph.D., author of *Brutal Virtue: The Myth and Reality of Banastre Tarleton* (2002).

>>>

This is an important work that furthers scholarship on Ferguson, his rifle, and the battle of Kings Mountain. The authors have combined historical research with archaeology and field testing to re-analyze several long standing myths and misconceptions about Ferguson and his rifle.

Robert M Dunkerly, author of *The Battle of Kings Mountain: Eyewitness Accounts*, and *The Kings Mountain Walking Tour Guide*

>>>

Bryan Brown and Ricky Roberts have compiled a definitive work on one of the American Revolution's more interesting characters, Patrick Ferguson, who developed the screw breech flint lock and commanded British riflemen in its use.

Bryan and Ricky have gone to the extra effort to authenticate every contemporary account, archeological findings and objects in museums from Ferguson's era.

James "Spot" Fulton

>>>

Review for
Every Insult and Indignity: The Life, Genius and Legacy of Major Patrick Ferguson

Although I've always primarily feasted on a steady diet of fiction novels I now and then find myself craving a revealing biography, or perhaps a really interesting and meaty morsel of history that tells a *true* story interwoven with fascinating facts I might not come across anywhere else. Not just a passing yen, it's a long-standing hunger for historical fact I've carried through the years for something that transcends anything ever offered way back in high school texts, which I unfortunately found very formal and dry (and which for the most part extinguished any enthusiasm I had then for American history.)

Ricky Roberts' and Bryan Brown's *Every Insult and Indignity* bestows all those good things I missed back then and more, plunging the lucky reader into a highly researched, multi-dimensional account of the true enigma of an unusual man by the name of Patrick Ferguson, his unique design for a military rifle that rocked the Revolutionary war, and modern misconceptions of the invention's effectiveness often due to error. (If only current political issues were so carefully and thoroughly examined!) The authors' passion for factual details along with their talent for crafting a compelling story have resulted in an absorbing book that anyone with a hankering for history will find highly satisfying, as I did.

--Leann Marshall, author of *The Starfish People* and *The Rendering*

>>>

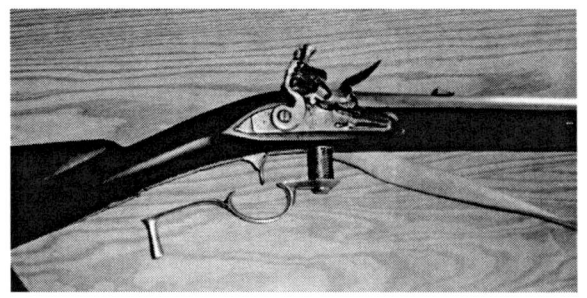

Every Insult and Indignity
The Life, Genius and Legacy of
Major Patrick Ferguson

An exploration into the care and feeding of
Patrick Ferguson's Breech-Loading Ordnance Rifle

Based on research using primary source historical documentation
and
validated by experimental archeology between 2005 and 2010

INCLUDING NEVER BEFORE SEEN EVIDENCE OF
FERGUSON'S BREECH-LOADING RIFLE
AT THE BATTLE OF KINGS MOUNTAIN

Ricky Roberts
&
Bryan Brown

ISBN-13: 978-1461158578

ISBN-10: 1461158575

First Edition August 2011

Printed in the United States of America on acid-free paper.
This book meets all ANSI standards for archival quality.

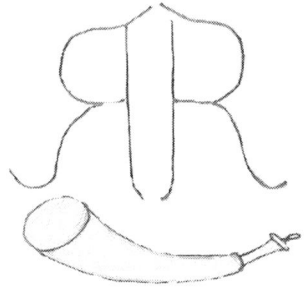

Ricky Roberts's cartouche stamp

Bryan Brown's cartouche stamp

A cartouche or stamp is commonly used to mark the work of artisans and tradesmen. As period artisans and historians, we feel that it is appropriate to "stamp" our work with our individual marks.

Table of Contents

Note to the Reader

The spelling and grammar used in the period documents included in this book has been retained from the original source. This may make the book more challenging to read, but we did not want to color the original with possibly erroneous modifications or interpretations. In addition, period quotes have been italicized to make them easily distinguishable from the general text.

All photographs and images in this book are from the collections of the authors, with the exception of those that are otherwise cited.

Disclaimer

In providing the information contained in this book to you, the authors and publisher make no warranty expressed or implied as to its validity or suitability. Any actions you take are solely your own responsibility. You are the guardian of your own safety and the safety of those around you.

YOU ARE THE ONLY SAFETY ON ANY FIREARM!

WE ARE DISCUSSING BLACK POWDER ARMS. UNDER NO CIRCUMSTANCES SHOULD YOU ATTEMPT TO USE SMOKELESS POWDER IN ANY BLACK POWDER ARMS!

Be smart, be safe!

Additional safety rules may be found in Appendix A

SAFETY FIRST!

If you are new to shooting live rounds from a black powder firearm, PLEASE find someone to show you how to properly and SAFELY load and shoot. We offer the following information only as a guide.

Safety classes can be located though:

The National Rifle Association (http://www.nra.org)

The National Muzzle Loading Rifle Association (http://www.nmlra.org)

Acknowledgments

The authors would like to thank all those who have helped and supported them throughout the evolution of this project.

Bryan would like to thank his wife, Shana, for her editing and input, love and support, and for her assistance and generosity which made this book possible. Let us be honest, in a just world her putting up with us through this process would make her eligible for sainthood.

We would like to thank Philip M. Edwards of Narragansett Arms, whose reproductions of the Ferguson Ordnance Rifle took the Ferguson Ordnance Rifle from an impossible dream to an achievable reality and his generosity in sharing pictures and research and resources with us.

We would also like to recognize the generous help and support we received from Bert Dunkerly, Katherine Lopez, and Chris Revels, all of whom are on the staff of the National Park Service at Kings Mountain National Military Park; Spot Fulton and John Braxton; the trustees and staff of the Tower of London Armoury Museum; Mike, Shannon and Jesse Mylotte at The Rifle Shoppe, Inc., the great folks at Track of the Wolf, Inc., and Chuck Dixon, his family and their custom Gunmaker's Fair. In addition we received assistance from the members of the Hesse Kassel Jaeger Korps, Joe Hinson, the members of the New Acquisition Militia, the members of the Widowmakers, the American Long rifle Association, the members of the National Rifle Association, the members of the National Muzzle Loading Rifle Association and the reenacting and muzzle loading community in general.

We also acknowledge the work and inspiration provided by the giants who came before us and whose works helped to educate and inspire us to keep looking, digging, asking questions and learning. These include authors, gunsmiths, and scholars such as Kit Ravenshear, Howard Blackmore, DeWitt Bailey, W. Keith Neal, M.

M. Gilchrist, John Braxton, Chuck Dixon, Peter Alexander, George Shumway, Joe Kindig, Anthony Scotti and many others. We strongly encourage you to either buy their works, or borrow them from your local library or a friend. Read them, enjoy the illustrations and gain insight from the valuable lessons contained therein. Learning is fun, and fun is infectious…catch it!

The Ferguson Ordnance Rifle

Introduction

Both authors are historical reenactors and amateur historians, with a bit of a bug for firelocks and an itch for Patrick Ferguson's Breech-Loading Ordnance Rifle, specifically. In an era when most arms were smoothbore and loaded from the muzzle, Patrick Ferguson, the second son of a Scottish jurist, and a young man fascinated by all things military, developed what is, in our opinion, the ultimate pre-cartridge firearm.

What, you may ask, is a reenactor? Reenactors are people who dress up, live, and generally represent a certain time period, often demonstrating the skills and life of that era at a historical site. They are also known as *living history interpreters*, *living historians*, and *experimental archaeologists*. Generally, they are unpaid volunteers with a strong personal interest in history. Most tend to evolve into something of a specialist in specific periods of time, regions, or technologies. They personally invest many hours researching and learning their periods utilizing old documents, journals and images, among many other sources. They communicate with and share resources with other history buffs, and travel to historic sites to help educate the public, often spending thousands of dollars on equipment and transporting their gear to and from various events throughout the country. Often they form companies or "units" that recreate a specific group from history, be it military or civilian. Some connect with specific historical sites, while others travel from site to site throughout the year helping to educate visitors. Their purpose and goal is to help you learn more about an era or a region, showing us that that history can be more than a series of dry, boring dates and names, but rather a fascinating action adventure, all the more appealing because of its authenticity.

Our story kicked off in 2005 when Ricky purchased a reproduction Narragansett Ferguson Ordnance Rifle #85 (the Rifle Shoppe, Inc. was the source for the parts Narragansett used for this

Ferguson's Ordnance Rifle) that was lying on a blanket at a shoot from a fellow whose parting comment was "Fouling locked it up too fast." Now, to be fair, the gun had changed hands a time or two before this, most likely between folks who were similarly frustrated. But Ricky had long been reading the accounts of Patrick Ferguson and his rifle while living in the Western Carolinas near Kings Mountain, South Carolina, where Major Ferguson fell and is buried.

Ferguson's name may be more familiar to people in North Carolina then to folks in other parts of the country. He was a Scottish-born British officer who served in the Americas during the Revolution who invented a breech-loading flintlock rifle for Light Infantry troops that was capable of firing farther, faster and longer than any other period firearm. Ricky did not feel the previous owners experience with the rifle matched the historical accounts of its performance at the demonstrations at Woolwich in Britain and in the field, here in the Americas.

Ricky is no novice; he has been reenacting and shooting black powder since the 1970s and is a former member of the U.S. International Muzzle Loading Team. He has also represented the United States at many international black powder competitions, shooting anything from a matchlock to a caplock both in long arms and pistols. He is a member of the New Acquisition Militia, The Widowmakers, Hesse Kassel Jaeger Korps, American Long Rifle Association, the National Muzzle Loading Rifle Association, and the National Rifle Association, and is a regular attendee of the NMLRA Friendship shoots. Ricky has been publishing articles on living history for many years in *On The Trail* magazine in his popular "Ramblings of a Shirt tailed Man" series.

Recognizing the futility of reinventing the wheel, Ricky began digging for information about the rifle that he had purchased, asking many questions of folks to get leads about period references, hints, tips and information. This was all in an effort to get to the bottom of the Ferguson Ordnance Rifle enigma: how to get the same performance found in the historical record from a modern reproduction arm. At one point in his research, Ricky was directed to Bryan Brown, when they were both reenactors at the Battle of

16

Huck's Defeat in Brattonsville, South Carolina, on opposing sides. Since Ricky portrays a Rebel/Patriot rifleman with the New Acquisition Militia, and Bryan is a founding member of the Hesse Kassel Jaeger Korps (a Crown/British forces Rifle unit brought over specifically to hunt American Riflemen), they realized that they had been shooting at each other for years, but had not crossed paths socially as of yet.

Bryan has been a reenactor since 1977, having portrayed a variety of periods both in the United States and in Europe. Prior to helping found the Hesse Kassel Jaeger Korps, Inc. in 1995, he had spent the previous six years with the Maryland-based 71st Regiment of Highland Foote, Inc., where he first began to seriously dig into Ferguson and his rifle. Bryan is also an armourer and gunsmith, having built and taught others to build hundreds of black powder arms, edged weapons, tools and accoutrements since the early 1980s. He has "something of a penchant for building oddball arms" and has amassed an ever-expanding library of history and historical arms-related resources; like many reenactors, he is something of a book junkie. He is a member of the Hesse Kassel Jaeger Korps, the National Muzzle Loading Rifle Association, the National Rifle Association, the Honourable Company of Horners, the American Long rifles, the Company of Military Historians. He also belongs to less formal groups of period gunsmiths and armourers and is a regular attendee of Chuck Dixon's Custom Muzzle Loading Faire in Kempton, Pennsylvania.

A long-lasting friendship sparked by a common interest was born that day in Brattonsville, South Carolina, one of the fruits of which is this book. Ricky and Bryan swapped emails, discussed books and period references for quite some time, and were energized by the inquiry, the search for answers and, frankly, the thrill of the hunt. Bryan was so animated by the research and work with Ricky on the Ferguson rifle (all the time droolingly enviously over Ricky's Ferguson Rifle) that his beloved wife Shana actually surprised him one year with an anniversary gift of a set of parts and castings from The Rifle Shoppe, Inc., so he could build his own. Now THAT is a LOVING wife and a good woman!

As we have traveled to various historical sites and shooting ranges while demonstrating the Ferguson Breech-loading Rifle, and on some occasions allowing reenactors and the odd special guest to fire one, more than one reenactor has jokingly commented that they should sell all their reenacting kit now, since they had now "done it all." The Ferguson is a rare breed, and to fire one is a unique experience.

To make sure that everyone can follow along with some of the terminology, let us make a quick level set. The following terms are mainly derived from the 18th century, which makes research all the more challenging since the meanings of some of the words have changed over time, or are now applied to different things in the 19th and 20th centuries.

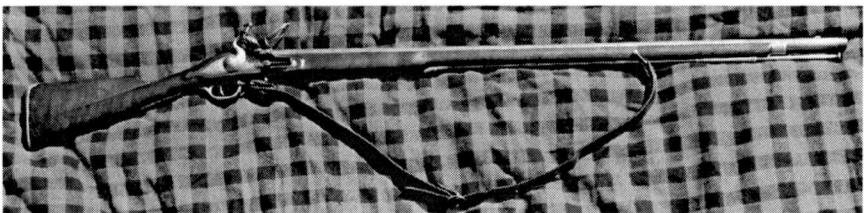

Short Land Pattern Musket, also known as the Brown Bess

- A MUSKET is a smoothbore military arm (it has no rifling—think shotgun in modern terms), generally in the .75 caliber range of bore size. It is always set up to mount a bayonet. Muskets tend to be very muzzle heavy due to their primary role as handles for bayonets. The heavier muzzle makes them thrust better with bayonets, and give mass to the parry of an opponent's bayonet. In the 18th century and in the British Army in particular the bayonet ruled the battlefield. The fact that the musket could fire was a bonus. It can fire single ball, multiple shot, or a mixture known as "buck and ball." A musket's effective range against a man-sized target is 80-90 yards.

1757 pattern Light Infantry Carbine

- A CARBINE is a smaller, lighter military arm than a full-sized musket. It is generally smoothbore, but is sometimes rifled. It is usually in the .62-.65 caliber bore range, and are usually set up to mount a bayonet, but it is balanced more for firing than for the thrust and parry of bayonet combat. This type of arm is commonly assigned to light infantry troops, artillery, or engineers/sappers. They can fire single ball, multiple shot, or the "buck and ball" mixture. The effective range of a carbine against a man-sized target is 70-80 yards.

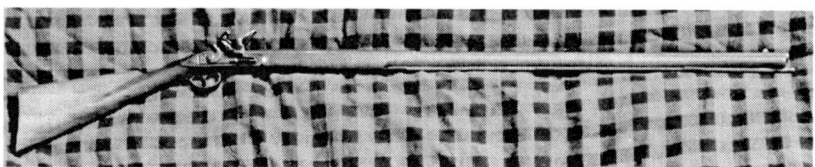

British Fowler

- A FUSIL (Fuzil, Fusee, Fuzee), and a Fowler are all generally smoothbore light hunting arms in the .62-.65 caliber range. These are civilian arms, although they are sometimes used in military service. You typically see these when militias press hunting arms into military service, or when officers and non-commissioned officers (NCOs) are looking for a lighter arm to take to the field. These military private purchase versions often fit a bayonet but are lighter than a carbine, and the bayonet is often more show than function. They can fire single ball, multiple shot, or the "buck and ball" mixture. A fusil's effective range against a man-sized target is 70-80 yards.

Pistor Jaeger Rifle

- A JAEGER or Jäger rifle is a larger bore rifle, commonly above .62 caliber; even .80 caliber is not historically uncommon. It is a shorter-barreled arms that use a Super Fine Double Strength glazed powder, which is more expensive and much stronger than standard musket powder. These rarely fit a bayonet in the 18th century. They generally fire a single ball, most often loaded with a leather or fabric patch to function as a gasket in their rifled barrel. A jaeger's effective range against a mansized target is 300-400 yards.

American Long rifle

- The AMERICAN LONG RIFLE is also referred to by some authors as a Kentucky or Pennsylvania Rifle, or as a Virginia or North Carolina rifle. For this discussion we will include all of the above-named American-made rifles in this genre. They tend to require a longer barrel to capture the energy of the slower burning, coarser standard grade musket powder that they use. The majority tend to be in the .40 -.58 caliber range, although there are exceptions in both directions. Their long, graceful stocks tend to be rather fragile for the rigors of military life. However, the longer sight plane (distance between front and rear sight) makes them excellent snap-shooting arms. They rarely fit a bayonet of any kind, and fire a single, generally patched ball. The Long rifle's effective range against a mansized target is 150-300 yards, depending in part on caliber—smaller calibers do not shoot as far as larger ones.

- MUZZLELOADERS and the vast majority of 18th century firearms load from the muzzle with loose powder and ball. In addition, loose powder is used as priming in the pan to facilitate firing. A well-drilled soldier with a musket or carbine can fire 3-5 rounds per minute. A rifle tends to fire 1-3 rounds per minute at best, since wooden ramrods load slower then metal ones, and tend to break more often.

Breech of breech-loading rifle

- BREECHLOADERS load at the breech, the closed end (when firing) of the barrel opposite the muzzle. Some have chambers that open, as is the case with the Ferguson Ordnance Rifle. Others, like the hackbuchshe, load with a replaceable chamber containing powder and projectile, and function somewhat as a very early precursor to metallic cartridges. Some are screw barrel breech-loaders, wherein the whole barrel screws off and is loaded and then screwed back onto the piece.

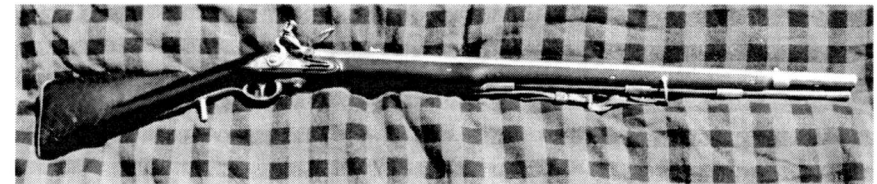

Ferguson Ordnance Rifle

- The FERGUSON ORDNANCE RIFLE is the specific military rifle designed and tested by Patrick Ferguson in the American colonies. Was the "Ferguson Rifle" the only one used? Not at all. There were a myriad of other military (many made for the East India Company militias) and civilian sporting models. The Ferguson Ordnance Rifle is a rapid firing breech-loading rifle made famous at the Battle of Brandywine. It was capable of firing 7 rounds per minute, engaging targets out to 300 yards, while loading on the move and in the prone position. When used with the proper period lubricants it will fire far more shots than any other period weapon without failure to fire due to fouling. And while the lines of the arm look like the Brown Bess musket, it is very much a rifle designed by a rifleman, and is well fit and balanced for shooting as its primary role, though it also mounted a bayonet.

- "period correct" is a term you will come across now and again in the manuscript that may be unfamiliar in concept. Historical reenactors as a whole tend to try to operate within period correctness, meaning that they use materials, tools and techniques appropriate to the period. They might eschew modern cartridge firearms or modern synthetic fabrics at an 18th century period event, for instance, because these items would not be correct materials or tools for the period in question, and therefore not "period correct." Items used inappropriately to the period are referred to as "farby" so the goal at all times is to be period correct.

The Ferguson Rifle is something of a Holy Grail type of quest for many Revolutionary War reenactors, the ultimate manifestation of 18th century arms-making gizmo worship. Building the Ferguson helped to give both Ricky and Bryan a greater insight into the technology and the genius of Patrick Ferguson and Durs Egg, the gunsmith who made the "better quality test pieces" at the Tower of London, and who is recognized as an exceptional genius and artisan in his own right. (Ask Bryan about the lock sometime; he will insist Durs Egg was an evil genius with that lock.)

But now let us move on with the meat of our tale.

The Inventor

Miniature c. 1774-1775 of Patrick Ferguson as Captain of a Light Infantry Company, 70th Regiment (*Image courtesy M.M. Gilchrist*)

British soldier Patrick Ferguson, born in June, 1744, died at King's Mountain. South Carolina on October 7, 1780. He was the son of James Ferguson, an eminent jurist, and a nephew of Lord Elibank. He was a true son of the heather, with family members on both sides of the 1745 Jacobite rebellion against British control of Scotland, including a relative sentenced to death for treason for plotting to abduct the king of England in support of Bonnie Prince Charlie. Pattie was not a claymore-swinging, kilted highlander, but rather grew up in the heart of the Scottish Enlightenment in his family's home in Edinburgh. His family is described as living "genteelly but with no extravagance"[1] as proper frugal Scots. Pattie's father James worked diligently during the Scottish Enlightenment to restore the family fortunes after being severely impacted by the South Seas Bubble economic crash of 1720. He also labored to clean the family of the stain of prominent Jacobite relatives in post-Jacobite "Enlightenment" Scotland.

Patrick was a complex and fascinating man who was prone to be misunderstood. These misunderstandings are exemplified by the errors that can be seen on his grave marker at Kings Mountain National Military Park.

TO THE MEMORY OF
COL. PATRICK FERGUSON
SEVENTY-FIRST REGIMENT,
HIGHLAND LIGHT INFANTRY.

BORN IN ABERDEENSHIRE,
SCOTLAND IN 1744.
KILLED OCTOBER 7,1780
IN ACTION AT
KINGS MOUNTAIN
WHILE IN COMMAND OF
THE BRITISH TROOPS.

A SOLDIER OF MILITARY
DISTINCTION AND OF HONOR.

THIS MEMORIAL
IS FROM THE CITIZENS OF
THE UNITED STATES OF AMERICA
IN TOKEN OF THEIR APPRECIATION
OF THE BONDS OF FRIENDSHIP AND
PEACE BETWEEN THEM AND THE
CITIZENS OF THE BRITISH EMPIRE.

ERECTED OCTOBER 7,1930

Patrick Ferguson's grave marker at Kings Mountain National Military Park

To the memory of
Col. Patrick Ferguson
Seventy-First Regiment.
Highland Light Infantry.
Born in Aberdeenshire
Scotland in 1744.
Killed October 7, 1780
in action at
Kings Mountain
while in command of
the British Troops.
A soldier of military
distinction and of honor.
This memorial
is from the citizens of
the United States of America
in token of their appreciation
of the bonds of friendship and
peace between them and the
citizens of the British Empire.
Erected, October 7, 1930.

Commissioned by R. E. Scoggins of Charlotte, North Carolina and dedicated by President Herbert Hoover in 1930, this marker, while well intentioned, perpetuates some common inaccuracies about Patrick Ferguson. He was a lieutenant colonel in the colonial militia, and as a regular army member of the 71st Highland Regiment of Foote (not the same as Highland Light Infantry raised in the 19th century) he was a major. Officers in the regular army were promoted one level when leading militia. This is understandable confusion, but one that typifies our misunderstanding of him, since his grave marker erroneously lists him as a full colonel in the 71st Foote.

Like his siblings and parents, Patrick was in all likelihood born in Edinburgh, not in Aberdeenshire. He was only thirty-six years old when he died on Kings Mountain, pierced by multiple rifle and musket balls, his clothes in tatters from near misses. His American adversaries, the Back Water Men (as the troops of the

Crown referred to them), or Over Mountain Men, (as the rebels called themselves) reportedly stripped his body and urinated on his corpse. Eventually, his aides were permitted to wash and bury his body, which was wrapped in a raw cowhide and buried in a shallow grave on the mountain. He was lowered into the ground alongside red-headed "Virginia Sal," one of two female refugees traveling under his command.

To this day the cairn (a man-made pile of stones) that marks his grave has a unique mythology associated with it. A cairn was commonly built on Scots graves to help protect the dead from animal scavengers; in fact, there is even a special breed of terrier to protect graves known as the *Cairn Terrier.* In Scottish tradition, placing a stone on the grave is also a mark of respect and remembrance. Conversely, in local folklore, Patriot forces have a tradition of putting the stones on the grave "to keep Ferguson in there." This is because Pattie remains as something of a boogeyman in the Western Carolinas, with parents and grandparents warning their children that "if you do not behave, Ferguson will get you." Folks that visit the site often pick up rocks while approaching his cairn to add to the stone pile. (While this is tempting, please do not do this. The National Park Service will just have to remove them to maintain the original cairn, and since they are nice, dedicated people, we don't want to make extra work for them).

Patrick Ferguson's grave marker and cairn at Kings Mountain National Military Park

Pattie, or "The Bulldog" as he was also known, was physically an elfin man—small and slight of stature—but huge in life and intellect. He was full of wit, humor and drive and, at one point in his travels, became so irritated with a London lady's utter ignorance about Scotland that he convinced her it was a country containing neither trees nor grass, but rather was completely covered with long coarse hair.[2]

He first entered military service with the 15th Regiment of Foote (a Scots Regiment in the English Establishment (standing army)) as an ensign at the tender age of twelve, but was recalled, due to his youth, as they were heading off to war. Later, at age fifteen, he purchased a cornetcy, the mounted equivalent of a lieutenant of infantry, in the Scots Grays' Dragoons. His uncle, General James Murray, Governor General of Quebec after James Wolfe, helped him get accepted into the Royal Military Academy at Woolwich, England, where Pattie studied for two years.

Later, Ferguson saw action in Germany during the Seven Years' War. We believe it may be here that he first became acquainted with breech-loading arms, in particular with the French Dragoons Chaumette-pattern arms. We know that he mailed a breech-loading pistol back to his family in 1775, most likely a Chaumette pattern. [3]

Other pistols figured prominently during his soldiering time in Germany. He dropped a pistol during one skirmish while jumping a ditch, and feeling that it was improper for a young officer to return without it, he turned around, jumped back over the ditch under fire, retrieved the pistol, and then returned, still under enemy fire, to his own lines.

At some point during his service in Germany, he seems to have injured his leg. Scholars believe that he caught synovial tuberculosis, a form of the disease that attacks the joints, most commonly the knees, as opposed to the lungs. Patrick was bedridden for six months while convalescing. The illness would trouble him for the rest of his life, affecting him so severely at times that he feared it would end his military career. His despair at this thought wrapped Pattie in what he referred to as the "sullens." The everyday life of a young officer in Edinburgh complicated his healing, with its mandatory parties, various social commitments and late evening socializing, all part of the "networking" of a career-minded young officer. However, with the nurturing of his maiden aunt, who lived in Buchan, some fresh country air, and time, he was able to regain his health. He was even able "to leap 10 feet" (his own foot length, not a twelve inch foot per se)[4], not leaping forward but bounding sideways. Patrick was ever the charming fellow with quite the silver tongue and the ability to bring people over to his point of view.

By 1765, his uncle offered to buy Pattie a captaincy in Canada, but his father was in ill health and he had to decline this generous offer. Before long the demands of a military career carried him away from his family, as his regiment, the Scots Greys, was posted in other parts of the United Kingdom. In 1768, Pattie purchased a captaincy of a company in the 70th Foot. This opportunity especially appealed to the frugal Scot, as it was a relatively cheap commission at the time. This was because the 70th was sailing for the West Indies, also ominously known as the "Fever Islands." Hardly the modern image of a tropical paradise, it was known as a place of slow lingering death from an assortment of miasma-borne diseases.

In the 18th century germ theory of disease did not exist. Instead, diseases were thought to be carried by vapors or noxious scents. One example of this was malaria, from the Latin *malus aria*, meaning "bad air." Most people in the period maintained heavy European dress, thinking it protected them from the vapors, though the resultant heat strokes did nothing to improve one's health prospects.

As implied above, the British Army in the 18th century was not a professional army in the modern sense. Commissions as officers were not based largely on education or merit, but on purchase and peerage. Most "promotions" were self-promotions in the most literal sense; you literally bought a higher rank, and sold off your lower rank to someone else in the process. In addition, you often tried to attain a rank that you could retire on by selling that commission. It was common for less career-minded officers to sell their commissions or exchange them for ones enabling them to remain in England and thus avoid harder, riskier duty. Nevertheless, the health risks stemming from either disease or battle rather improved ones chances of promotion by creating more turnover in the command structure. If you died, the commission returned to the regiment and the commander either sold it or granted it to someone else.

Originally, only nobility or peers had funds to be able to function within this system. With the beginnings of the Industrial Revolution the increase in wealth created a middle class of merchants and skilled workers whose families could afford to purchase these commissions, a type of free spending that went along with their bigger than life lifestyle. Encouraging nobles to keep up a flamboyant lifestyle was one of the ways a monarch kept them too impoverished to make much trouble, and this produced many peers willing to sell commissions to the highest bidder.

We know that while serving in Trinidad and Tobago, Pattie had access to Bidet, Hirst, and Willet pattern breech-loaders. He also purchased breech-loading rifles made from John Wassup's pattern, wherein the breech plug was completely removed with a wrench while opening a hole in the underside of the barrel. While Pattie was serving in Grenada in 1770, he requested that Durs Egg make several Wassup pattern rifles for Ferguson with the breech plug attached to the trigger guard instead of using a separate wrench. It still had traditional screw threads and required twelve turns to open the breech, but the evolution of the Ferguson Ordnance Rifle had begun.[5]

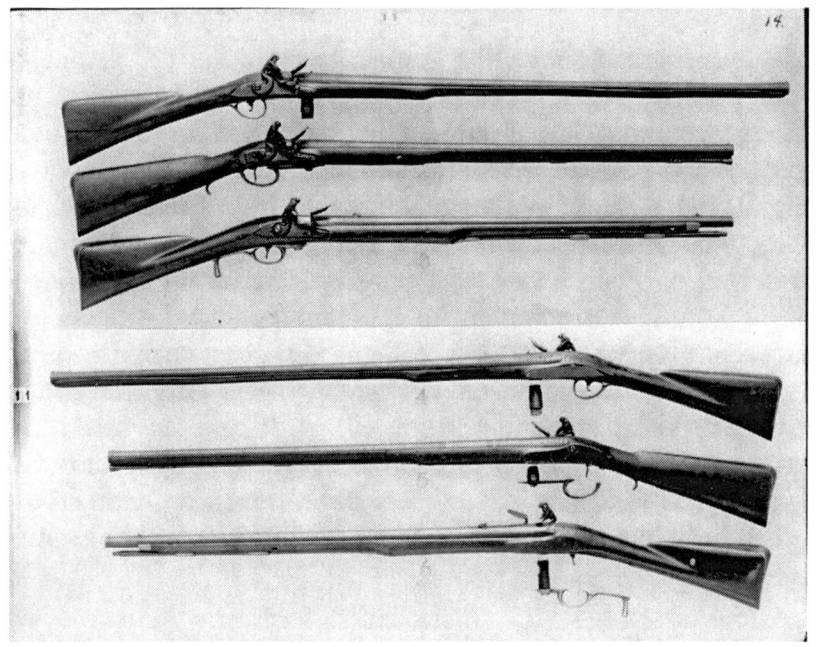

Hirst, Bidet and Ferguson rifles (*Image courtesy of Milwaukee Public Museum*)

He was most excited at this opportunity to serve overseas since it provided an opportunity to make his fortune and pursue his military career. In a letter to his sister, he wrote:

Do you know who writes this Bess? The very Respectable Captain Patrick Ferguson of the 70th Regiment. Between you & I bess I have got a very good Company, in a very good Regiment, very cheap. but as to last part of the story the less said about it the better. as the Cheapness of a purchase may take of from future Claims. By the Lord my Pen will not deign to touch the paper, my toes the Ground, nor will I have one clear Idea these three Months. I coud have hug'd Lord Barington the Secretary at war for My Commission. I will probably have the honor of Kissing the kings hands & I will do it sincerely, for I mean to serve him Bess, & it shall be the ruling principal of my life to be always in Opposition to - Opposition to my King, particularly when he is in the Right, when he is the most virtuous Man of his dominions, & plagued by a set of hellhounds - so for politicks.[6]

Pattie was a practical, frugal man who took the responsibilities of command and the health and welfare of his men most seriously:

My Command lays here & will find me employment enough. This Climate makes the men Indolent; Indolenc[e] produces dirt, Sickness, relaxation of Discipline & in short is ruin to the troops. -

My sole nostrum is exercize & occupation, tho this Climate will not Admit of too large dozes: I will make men & Soldiers of them at the same time; but what is all this to you? –

I left Granada about a fortnight ago & do not propose to return soon. - All west india Climates are alike to me, & actualy seem to improve my Constitution. I have been in five Different Islands & have enjoy'd uncommon good health in them all: I cannot however say that our men so are healthy as at home, owing I am convinced to the necessity they are

*under of eating Salt provisions & the Excesses they
are apt to indulge themselves in with new rum which
is the only kind they can well Afford to purchase. The
Officers however are as healthy as can be imagined
& after the first month or two few of them have had
even a headache, but of their own procuring. -*

*I propose to counteract in some degree the
effects of the Salt provisions by establishing a garden
for the Men & forcing the lazy Dogs to cultivate it; as
I have a hundred Acres of Government land at my
Disposal. It is strange that the Officers who have
commanded the troops here these three years have
never thought of this recourse in a part of the world
where there is no possibility of procuring garden
Stuff by other means.*[7]

While serving in the Fever Islands, Pattie purchased an estate there with the intention of growing sugar cane, even going so far as to refer to himself as "Laird" upon occasion. But his heart was not in it, and he eventually left the administration of the estate to his brother, George, who later served as the island's governor. Their uncle Sandy described Patrick as *"a little military mad, and infinitely more calculated to that profession than to the planting of canes"*[8]

Patrick sailed back to the British Isles in 1772, and attended Lord General Howe's Light Infantry School in 1774. During his studies he showed a real talent for light infantry tactics and became a strong proponent of drilling light troops to a silver whistle. Lord General William Howe, Commander-in-Chief of the Crown forces in the Americas, would remember this young officer's zeal for *La Petite Guerre* later on when he would require his skills to quell the looming troubles in the colonies.

In 1775, as the British Army began to tool up for an almost inevitable war with the Americans, young Captain Patrick Ferguson of the 70th Regiment of Foot had the idea to supply the army with an advanced breech-loading rifle to counter the threat of the dreaded American Long rifle. Also known as the Widow Maker, the

American Long rifle was understandably feared by British officers who had heard stories of sharpshooters specifically targeting officers, and tales of the incredible shooting skill attributed to the American riflemen. The Crown responded by deploying specialized rifle troops, such as the Hessian Jaegers and Ferguson's Experimental Company, among several others. After repeated demonstrations of his Ordnance Rifle for fellow officers, general staff, and finally for the king himself, Pattie's idea was accepted, and he started building production prototypes, engaging several local London gunsmiths to do so.

Patrick Ferguson did not invent the screw breech breechloader Henry the VIII favored in the 15th century for bird hunting on his estates. The patent he took out on December 2nd, 1776 was for "improvements on the breech-loading rifle." Thus he did not originate the concept, but did make refinements to the design.

The Ferguson rifle was the end result of much hard work, requiring several prototype versions to be built by unknown gun makers prior to Pattie approaching Durs Egg. As the famed Swiss gunsmith to the king and master at the Tower of London Armoury, Egg was asked to build better quality rifles for the various tests that the weapon was soon to endure.

At this period an improved rifle was just being brought to the attention of the military authorities. Major Patrick Ferguson (of King's Mountain fame), egged on by the boasted skill of the American marksmen, had invented a breech-loader. The breech was opened by a screw plug to allow admission of ball and cartridge; special arrangements were made to prevent the fouling of the plug and the accumulation of gas, and the piece was sighted for one hundred to three hundred yards. In June, 1776, he gave a demonstration at Woolwich before Lord Amherst, Viscount Townshend, General Harvey, and several other prominent officers. He astonished the beholders. "Notwithstanding a heavy rain and a high wind, he fired," according to a contemporary, ". . .

after the rate of four shots per minute at a target two hundred yards distant. He next fired six shots in one minute. He also fired (while advancing after the rate of four miles per hour) four times in the minute. He then poured a bottle of water into the pan and barrel of the piece when loaded, so as to wet every grain of powder; and in less than half a minute, he fired with her, as well as ever, without extracting the ball. Lastly, he hit the bull's eye, lying on his back on the ground. Incredible as it may seem to many, considering the variation of the wind, and wetness of the weather, he only missed the target three times, during the whole course of the experiment.[43]

Ferguson took out a patent for his improvements, and was allowed to form a corps of riflemen composed of volunteers from regiments serving in America. While rifled flintlocks were not officially adopted by the regular army [end of sentence]

An excellent marksman, Patrick was familiar with the vertical breechloading mechanism designed over 50 years before by Issac De la Chaumette. It was sometimes used in sporting rifles, but not by the army. The regulation 'Brown Bess' smooth-bore musket loaded at the muzzle. Yet breech-loaders would enable soldiers to reload quickly, while lying prone or without breaking cover; rifling would improve accuracy of aim over greater distance. Chaumette's mechanism, modified by Georges Bidet, tended to foul, with powder clogging the threads of the breech plug.[9]

...He adapted the design of the breech-block and the plugs threading to minimize fouling, adding a grease-groove, and also a folding rear-sight. At his own expense he had prototypes made and began testing.[10]

Four shots a minute is an impressive number in and of itself for a period arm, especially in foul weather. General Hervey, watching Pattie's demonstration for the general staff officers, commented that the weather was "a bad day for your show," to which Pattie is reported to have replied, "On the contrary, sir, a splendid day to show you what I have in mind."[11]

In the muzzle-loading/black powder era keeping your powder dry could mean the difference between life and death. With muzzle-loading arms, becoming fouled with wet powder was a major problem which could easily result in wasting half an hour to pull a ball from the muzzle clear and reload a standard issue musket. This process often required several people and/or specialized tools to accomplish. Patrick Ferguson was able to do this with his weapon in half a minute, a truly impressive aspect which never fails to impress black powder shooters when we demonstrate this particular feature.

Ferguson's Uncle Jamie served with Lord Townsend during the Quebec Campaign and introduced him to his nephew. Here is an excerpt from Patrick Ferguson's letter to Lord Townsend, Master General of Ordnance, Colonel in Chief of the Royal Regiment of Artillery:

> *But My Lord I here present your Lordship with an arm which fires with twice the Expidition & five times the certainty, it is several pounds lighter and requires only a forth part of the Powder of a common firelock, as can be testify'd by many officers in town who have repeatedly seen it at a Considerable distance throw five balls into a small mark in a minute, where as you have not a man in your army who will fire a musket half so quick and scarce put every fifth ball into a target at that distance- I shall only say that I will undertake to have the arms to be ready to be thrown into America before the arrival of your Germans, without interfering wit your other operations" April 1776* [12]

The comment on the "forth part" powder would seem to indicate a charge of approximately 65 grains if the "common firelock" in question had a 300-yard range like the Ferguson

Ordnance Rifle, e.g. an Amusette or wall gun. If that is what he is referring to, the math works out nicely. If it is a Brown Bess or Long Land Pattern Musket reference, then the comment is a trifle exaggerated.

> *June 1776*
> *In Birmingham he supervised the manufacture of the first Ferguson rifles made for military service. The contracts had been given to Barker & Whatley, Galton & Sons, William Grice, Benjamin Willets each to make 25 rifles.* [13]

Ferguson also reported a number of private orders for his rifles, including eighteen for General Frazier, who wanted to equip his officers and NCOs out of his own pocket.[14] Through Lord Germain General Frazier also requested the Crown to equip his two light companies with Ferguson's rifles.

With interest from the East India Company to purchase arms made to his design and gunsmiths already copying it to compete for the East India business, Pattie tried throughout the winter to secure a patent for his rifle.

> *My Rifle is in a fair way—by the unanimous suffrages of every officer who has seen it, has it been recommended as superior to any Musket Rifle or other fire arm now in use, & Lord Townsend now talks of having some hundreds made.*
> *Every defect is now got the better off, & those very faults which serv'd as Jibs to the whole being now corrected, I have nothing to fear. As to promotion, I do not expect any; & yet I think something may be perhaps done, If I was supported by any Interest. I mean if possible to attract his Majestys attention next Week, & as my Labors have been very disinterested, perhaps if properly supported I might get rank. I write Jamie on this subject this night & shall be obliged to you to enquire whither or not he receives my Letter. I have declined every kind of Interest untill*

the merit of my invention should make its own way - that time is now arrived, & freinds may be of most essential use - I wish to be introduced to his Majesty, which the Privy Seal can easily bring about, & then if I am thought to deserve it rank may be allow'd me, if I meet with support. -
I am almost decided to take out a patent. I foresee that the East India Company, the west India Militias, as well as the army & Militias at home will come into it, & it is only £70 ventured for a great Object. - altho the invention is not entirely my own, yet its application to the only Arm where it can be of use is mine, & moreover there are several original improvements (without which it will not Answer) which are entirely mine. - I shall also have the Custom of all nick-nacky People & Gentlemen who have deer parks or keep Game keepers in the Highlands.[15]

Having funded all the trials and test from his own pay, he was running up debts of £8 to £10 per month by December, 1776. Room and board in London was expensive and he had to economize:

…by means of my lodging and servant washing &c: my subsistence which 7/6 per day is swollow'd up nearly by the time I have eat my breakfast
…a tavern I never enter & can scarce a afford a coffee house dinner every other day[16]

Wed 19 Feb 1777 [in a letter to his sister] *Genl: Harvey told me that his Majesty had directed him to propose to me to go to America-'was I willing?' 'certainly to go where his Majesty pleases' – a report was accordingly made to the King, & orders issued for forming a Company of 100 Men from the Chatham recruits for that Service, to embark as this Day- the warning was short, the Command not very flattering for an Old Capt.n of 18 years Service, & I had been Obliged to take whatever Men were* *pointed out to me- they have neither Cloathes for that Service, nor are in any respect to my wish"………. I shall endeavour to have 60 men more (which there are rifles for) thrown into the same ship……………<snip>   ………The   King proposes giving me £100 to equip me* [17]

What Makes The Ferguson So Unique?

Some authors belittle Patrick Ferguson and begrudge the English patent office for issuing a patent on his new design, citing similar components that were used by other contemporary gun makers, instead of taking all Pattie's ideas into account. However, no other arm has all of these improvements applied collectively to one weapon:

- One significant change was to design a breech system with eleven (twelve on civilian models) "starting" threads, instead of simple threads, as with previous inventors. Each thread makes two full rotations around the breech plug. This allows the breech to open in *one full rotation* instead of the four rotations, as required in Chaumette's or Bidet's designs, or completely removing it, as with Wassup's/ Warsop's design, which Ferguson used in the Caribbean earlier in his career. Was Pattie the first to use starting threads? No, he was not, but he significantly improved upon their design.

- Pattie added *anti-fouling cuts* to the breech screw to force the debris left behind after shooting black powder out of the way of the threads. It was pushed either into the reservoir at the back of the breech or into the rear of the firing chamber where it could be burned by follow-on shots.

- Whereas some earlier breech-loaders used cylindrical breech plugs that were more susceptible to fouling, the *11-degree taper to the breech plug*, also known as a Morse taper, makes it less prone to fouling. Some argue that screws were impractical in the period with "all being hand cut" with a file, but this simply is not the case. Denis Diderot's *Encyclopédie, ou dictionnaire raisonné des sciences, des arts et des métiers (Encyclopedia, or a systematic dictionary of the sciences, arts, and crafts)* shows that the technology and tooling for making the quick or starting threads dates from at least the year 1763.

- The powder chamber in a Ferguson *is tapered*, whereas some earlier breechloaders used cylindrical chambers that were more susceptible to fouling and did not center the ball as well on the rifling.

- Pattie also recognized that one of the weaknesses of most rifles of his era was their inability to mount a bayonet. So he made certain that his rifle had the ability to do so. His rifle was equipped with a long sword bayonet, that some historians have attributed to a vitriolic mythological hatred of the American cause, but which could not be farther from the truth. The Ferguson Ordnance Rifle with its mounted bayonet is the same length tip to butt as a Brown Bess or Charleville musket mounting its bayonet. It is a matter of reach, or, as we say in our presentations, "If you are in a fight that comes down to a pointy thing on the end of a stick, you don't want to be the one with the short stick."

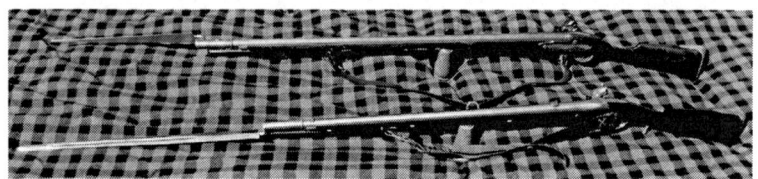

Ferguson (top) Short Land Pattern Musket "Brown Bess" (bottom)

Patrick Ferguson's Patent

While some attempt to discredit or dismiss Ferguson as not inventing the breech-loader, he never specifically made such a claim; he merely tried to improve upon already existing designs. However, what he did patent was an incredible jump in the practicality of a breech-loader in the pre-cartridge era with his *"Improvements in Breech-loading Fire-arms."*

A.D. 1776 . . . . N⁰ 1139.

Ferguson's Improvements in Breech-loading Fire-arms.

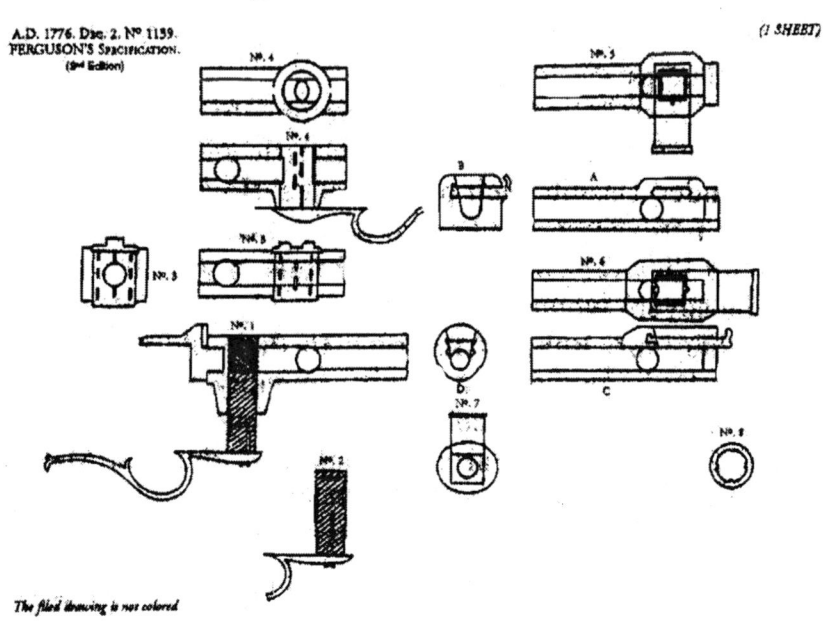

Patrick Ferguson's Patent *(Public domain image)*

An Essay on Shooting in 1789 by John Acton

By far the most expeditious way of charging rifled pieces, however, is by means of an ingenious contrivance which now generally goes under the name Ferguson's Rifle Barrel, from it's having been employed by Major Ferguson's Corps of rifleman during the last American war. In these pieces, there is a [round] opening on the upper part of the barrel, close to the breech, which is [just] large enough to admit the ball. This opening is filled by a rising screw [of which the trigger guard is the handle] which passes up from the underside of the barrel, and has it's threads cut with so little obliquity that when screwed up [to close the hole], a half-turn sinks the top of it down to a level with the lower side of the caliber [i.e. flush with the bottom of the bore]. The ball is put into the opening from above [and] runs forward a little way; the powder is then poured in so as to fill up the remainder of the cavity, and a half turn brings up the screw again, cuts off any superfluous powder, and closes up the opening through which the ball and powder were put. The chamber where the charge is lodged is without rifles [i.e. rifling], and so somewhat wider than the rest of the bore, so as to admit a ball that will not pass out of the barrel without taking on the figure of the rifles, and acquiring the rotary motion when discharged.[18]

We know Pattie was aware of other breech- loading arms, and that he had a low opinion of double barrel guns:

I have sent down in the Freindship *George Ritchie Master for Leith one Gun Case containing two Double barrel'd Guns, directed for the Hon:*ble *Lord Pitfour at Edinburgh: if his Lordship should not want them both be so good as send the one to M*r *Ross of Pitcalny, & the other may remain in your House for*

Captain Henderson at Logie near Sterling, to whom I shall write to apply to you for it. The Price of the Guns is five Guineas each, and five shillings more for <u>each</u> on Account of Bullet Moulds, worms, box, Carriage & sending on board, to which you will add, the Ship Charges.

- The Guns are plain, but Serviceable, Stub barrels well proved & shoot tollerably, but not so well as they would have done before the Barrels were brazed together which plays the Devil. You will think them too heavy, but I never will be concern'd in ordering a light Gun, which is a bauble & the difference of weight will not be felt the 2^d Day. -

In the Same case I have sent down the pistol which loads at the breech, which you will send home with my Compliments.[19]

Ferguson's Letter regarding Lord Townsend, Master General of Ordnance

When laying out this book, we had planned on adding a section for the discussion of Patrick Ferguson's efforts to have his rifle presented to the king and, hopefully, being employed in the army. We decided, however, to let Pattie tell you about the process in his own words, since he tells the story with his own style and clarity. In a letter to his sister, he explains:

My Reception here has not been such as a projector would have wish'd. Genl: Harvey is cautious of interfering with Ordnance Matters, & indeed has scarce taken time to look into the Merits of the Arm. I have however been with Lord townsend by his desire, & had this Day two hours conversation about it. They have so much ado just now in making Stoppers, brushes, Pickers $&^c$ $&^c!$ that it is impossible to take any new thing in hand. But My Lord I here present your Lordship with an arm which fires with twice the Expidition, & five times the certainty, is several pounds lighter & requires only a *fourth part of the Powder of a common firelock, as can be testify'd by many officers in town who have repeatedly seen it at a Considerable distance throw five balls into a small mark in a minute, where as you have not a man in your army who will fire with a musket half so quick & scarce put every fifth ball into a target at that distance - I shall only say my Lord that I will undertake to have the arms ready to be thrown into america before the arrival of your Germans, without interfering with your other operations - Another time we will think of it. I do not desire you my Lord, the Invention will make its own way, & will not be overlook'd; I am only solicitous that we may avail ourselves of the Advantage of it, before the present critical Occasion, before it comes into general use.*

Such has been my conference with this Man of War, in the mean time every person who has see the Execution & Expedition of my rifle, has been astonish'd at it, & they have join'd with one voice for the Necessity of Employing it. - I am much obliged to you for your kind Anxiety about my firing & the Success of the rifle. It is indeed most freindly - It will give you pleasure to know that I have ascertain'd firing, so as never to make a bad shot: tho certai[nly] some Days better, Some Worse. however [paper torn] worst firing, join'd to my Expedition makes them Stare here, & I now make known my practising Days, that the world may do justice to an improvement, that is in danger of being over look'd, least there should not be a Sufficiency of Stoppers & Pickers! -

All I ask is that they will see the Gun fire & if it then proves equal to my description that they will allow me 6 men for a fortnight to practice with & if at the end of that time they do not put more balls into a target in equal times & distance than any 24 in your Army give up all thoughts of it - It is the only project I ever hear'd of that is to be indisputably ascertaind in a fortnight without any expence. But they will blush for this ere long. [20]

46

Report of Patrick Ferguson's Demonstrations for the King at Woolwich

London Octr 2.^{d} 1776

Yesterday I had the honor of exhibiting various experiments with my Rifle Gun before their majesties in Windsor forrest, which happened in the following manner. Knowing that the King retires there three days every week & having some acquaintances in the Reg.^{t} which mounts guard upon him I proposed to Fotheringham (Pouries Son Macleods Nephew) who happens to command there, that I would bring down some rifles & teach his men the use of them, in hopes that his Majesty might hear of them. Fother.^{m} of course was glad of the opportunity & so set out last friday morning. I had only been three days at work with my Disciples when yesterday morning I had a message from the King by Col. Egerton to inform me that his Majesty meant to see them at five in the afternoon. Altho' my Six associates were by no means masters of their business, yet the three days practice had made them at least a match for four times their number of Grenadiers so I took the field with a tolerable opinion of my Troops and some confidence in my own Generalship At the hour appointed their Majestys came arm & arm into the field & as the design had been keept secret they were not troubled with mob. I begun by making the men fire at a Target at 100 y.^{ds} As they were alarmed by the Kings presence they did not acquit themselves so well as they had done by themselves, but still well enough to shew the Rifle. After they had finished I took the liberty of observing to his maj^y that the soldiers were more disturbd by his presence than they would have been by that of their enemy. When I was proceeding to fire his Majesty askd me how many shots I could fire in a minute. I answered that I had fired 7. He said Lord Townsend had told him so I took the liberty of adding that altho I could fire that number of random Shots yet I *could not undertake to bring down above five of his Majesties Enemys in that time. He laughd very heartily & went back to the Queen who was some paces behind & upon his repeating this there was a second general laugh. His majesty had express'd uneasiness whilst the men were firing at some people who were standing within a few y.^{ds} of the mark. I took the liberty of assuring H. M. that I would without hesitation stand within a yard of it, and after they had had a fortnights practice offered to hold the Target in my hand. he said it was better let alone I fired nine shots viz. three upon my back and the other six as fast as I could standing and put five balls into the black Spot and the other four within four inches of it. The Emperor of Germany would have given me a Diploma constituting me Archrifleman throughout his Empire had I done this with the assistance of the best rest and taking five minutes to each shot. I felt that it was impossible to fire ill before the King, but this was beyond my hopes. This was done in less than two minutes. The king was pleased afterwards to examine my equipment, as well as a dress calculated for Service which I had brought into the field upon another man on purpose and after considering the lightness certainty and expedition of my Rifle Gun with the quantity of amunition a man could easily carry he was pleased to observe in my hearing "he is an army in himself" I had mentioned to him, that to have balls go with truth & force, they require to be smaller than the bore of the Gun & that untill this method of loading occurred, the loss of time more than counterbalanced that advantage but that now we had the certainty of the one with double the expedition of the other. He conceived my meaning instantly (which not one man in a thousand would have done) and explaind it to those about him, before he left the field he expressed the highest approbation; observing that some had objected to this new invention, but that he saw every thing for it, and nothing agt it. He afterwards ask'd Col. Egerton if I was not Genl Murrays Nephew & told him I had been* *recommended to him by Gen.[1] Howe when with the Light Companys at Salisbury I took the liberty of presenting the King with a Sketch & description of the rifle Gun, in which its advantages are touched upon in as few words as I could contrive.*[21]

Replicating the Tests at Woolwich

In our research and testing of the Ferguson Ordnance Rifle we set out to attempt to recreate Ferguson's demonstration at Woolwich for the British General Staff and for King George III. For a successful test, we wanted to meet the following criteria, and to be able to do so consistently and repeatedly:

- Nine shots - At least six offhand shots in two minutes with no less than five in the black
- Load, prime, dump in a canteen of water, and begin firing again within one minute or less
- Load and fire while kneeling
- Load and fire prone

   " I begun by making the men fire at a Target at 100 yds   *"*[22]

   " I fired nine shots viz. three upon my back and the other six as fast as I could standing and put five balls into the black Spot and the other four within four inches of it. The Emperor of Germany would have given me a Diploma constituting me Archrifleman throughout his Empire had I done this with the assistance of the best rest and taking five minutes to each shot. I felt that it was impossible to fire ill before the King, but this was beyond my hopes. This was done in less than two minutes. "[23]

These quotes appear to describe firing offhand and 18th century prone (on one's back, or supine, as opposed to the 21st century interpretation, which is lying face down).

If we take surviving information and examples for 100-foot targets to derive modern 100-yard targets we believe they would be a 9-inch diameter black ring, 18-inch diameter red ring, and 39-inch green ring.

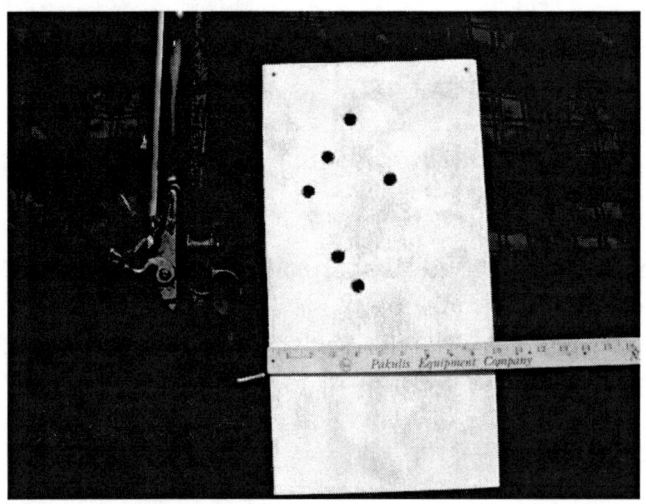

Ricky's demonstration target—10 x 19 inches, shot at 100 yards, 1 minute 20 seconds, 6 rounds fired.

Using the late Howard Hill's archery axiom—"aim small…miss small,"—Ricky thought he could improve his 100-yard group by decreasing the size of the target; the new target was 10 x 19 inches. He decided to use Patrick Ferguson's suggested half-a-dozen balls mentioned in his Woolwich quote. It took Ricky one minute and twenty seconds to fire these six quickly-aimed shots in the offhand stance. As can be seen in the above illustration, this target is a testament to the Ferguson Rifle's accuracy and rate of fire, which could not be matched by any other firearm of the 18th century.

The following plates are from an 1804 edition of author Ezekiel Baker's *Twenty-Three Years Practice and Observation with*

Rifle Guns.[24] Since this is a bit after the period we are examining, the uniforms shown are Napoleonic rifle uniforms, but the firing positions are those demonstrated by Patrick Ferguson for the king at Woolwich.

Rifleman standing, offhand position (*Public domain image*). Note that a sling was used to brace the firing arm.

Rifleman firing kneeling (*Public domain image*)

Rifleman firing from his belly (*Public domain image*)

Ignore the Napoleonic period hat used in the illustrations. During the American Revolution, a backpack or handy log would have been just as practical. This 'technique' of shooting was a selling point for this stiff hat.

Rifleman firing from his back. This is the position referred to as "prone" in the 18th and 19th centuries, versus the belly down position that currently comes to mind. (*Public domain image*)

Ferguson and his Rifle Come to America

First physical evidence of Ferguson Rifle in the Americas. This was recovered by Charlie Salerno in Long Island, New York. *(Image courtesy Charlie Salerno)*

Patrick Ferguson brought his Experimental Rifle Company to the American Colonies in March of 1777. He reported to the Ordnance Store Keeper, (similar to a supply office in modern military terminology) in New York City:

26 Mar 1777

Ltr to the Board with a Certificate of the Number of Rifle Guns produced here by Cptn Ferguson of the 70th Regiment together with a copy of his Letter of the 23rd Inst respecting Powder Flasks. Rifle Guns 67 Bayonets[33]

There was a shortage of powder flasks at the time; in fact, there were less than even this small number of Rifle Guns.[25] He did not yet have all 100 rifles, only having 67 at this point, and he doesn't even have enough powder flasks for those 67 rifles.

There is evidence that an additional 33 rifled guns were completed and shipped to the Americas, but there is no indication that they ever reached Ferguson.[26]

May-June 1777

We who belong to the Light Troops sometimes come into sight of them, & exchange a few distant innocent Shots- My Lads were only concern'd in one Skirmish in a wood, where we had Six kill'd & wounded as they have never exceeded 90 under arms, it is a slice from my small command which I can ill afford

The two quotes from Ferguson's letters to home put the number of men in the unit at between sixty and ninety. His use of the term "under arms" versus commenting upon his rifles in particular makes one suspect that some of his men may have carried muskets. We have not found concrete evidence that more than the 67 rifles he had on hand when he embarked for American shores ever actually reached his company. Therefore, we do not know if his command was entirely armed with the Ferguson Rifle or a mixture of arms, including muskets and/or carbines. On July 4, 1777, while in the American colonies, he tested the artillery piece he had designed based on the same technology as his rifle. Unfortunately it failed and exploded due to an iron barrel and over-sized ball. Consequently he ordered others made with bronze (brass) barrels, but there is no record that he ever received them. This is important for two reasons. First, we know the artillery did not ship with him when he left England; and secondly, this may be the strongest evidence that he may have had his full 100 rifles.

Some historians from the 19th and 20th centuries took great lengths to vilify Patrick Ferguson, painting him as some sort of rabid, tyrannical lunatic bent on the wholesale slaughter of the American colonists. This could not be farther from the truth. Only about one-third of colonists were pro-Congress (Whig)/anti-King George III, about the same amount fervently pro-King/anti-Congress (Tory). The rest were neutral, or their political allegiances may have swayed depending on who was encamped in their immediate neighborhood. Most people simply wanted to be left alone to support their families and pursue their livelihood. Pattie had no tolerance for abuse of the colonists or their families, but alternately had no love for those he saw as traitors. In a letter to Alexander Scrymgeour, written across several days between 29 June 1777—8 July 1777, while engaged in operations between Amboy, New Jersey and Staten Island, New York he stated:

> *In the Skirmish abovemention'd the rebells very soon Sicken'd, (altho in their favorite Ground,) - & left us. - they are not very Generous, & of Course the troops have adopted their Manners - two days ago, my company forming the rear Guard, We employd ourselves for two hours in Saving a family from being pillaged by the Hessians; with that view we remain'd rather long, & in a minute afterwards 3 Shot were fired at a Sergeant & me who were a few yards behind from the House - they fire most infamously ill - I return'd one Shot upon which the man (who was behind a tree) drop'd, & a 2d was Shot two minutes after by four of my people; so their virtue was rewarded. The night before last, I placed a guard to protect the furniture & Stock of a seemingly well disposed family, whilst the man of the house was employ'd in informing our Enemys, & his Sons in conducting some riflemen upon my Post. We paid more than they ask'd for everything to make up for the little Pillage which we could not prevent, & the Scoundrel was secured as a traytor before we had been a Quarter of an hour out of his house.*[27]

Ferguson was appalled when the rebels shot at the king's men with their paroles still in their pockets, considering it a lack of honor on their parts. These were serious breaches of the Articles of War, offenses punishable by immediate execution as a traitor. Having a "parole" meant a man had already been captured bearing arms against the king, and had been given another chance if he promised to return home to take care of his family and abstain from taking up arms for the duration of the war.

To George Ferguson, 8 October 1777, Wilmington,
Delaware - 21 January 1778, Philadelphia

Our Soldiers irritated by the duplicity, treachery and
the base Cruelty of the Inhabitants of the Jerseys
(Who have been repeatedly detected in firing at our
Centrys with the Gener:.^{ls} Protections in their pockets
&.^{c}) had taken libertys there which the General was
always averse to and had it particularly at heart to
put a Stop to upon our entering a new Country: and
as every man of common humanity must be happy in
exherting himself for so virtuous a purpose, you may
believe I obey'd his Commands with diligence and
alacrity and I have the Satisfaction of knowing that I
have protected a number of innocent familys from
outrage of other Corps and that not a Soldier of my
detatchment has been detected in marauding whilst
under my Command - and by God I will never Suffer
it or Serve in an Army where it is allow'd.[28]

Ferguson was frustrated by the unwillingness of the
American rebels to follow the recognized Articles of War, with their
allowance of parole and limited war. The American rebels were
colloquially referred to as "brother Jonathan" by the British, since
they were still viewed as British subjects, and the Crown did not
want to indulge in the total war that surely would have followed on
the European Continent. Although the British solders lived off of the
land while destroying all the enemy farms and livestock in the
process, the Crown did not actually want to inflict this sort of
devastation on what they saw as their own colonies populated by
their own people.

These frustrations colored Patrick Ferguson's dealing with
Congressional troops and irregular militia throughout the rest of the
war, leading up to his death at Kings Mountain. The war in the
American colonies, especially in the South, was as much a civil war
as a war of rebellion, with brother fighting brother. In some regions

it was also a religious war. Its brutality can be exemplified by the case of one Captain Sherrill, a militia officer in the Carolinas, who rode two horses to death trying to get to the Battle of the Waxhaws, all in an effort to have an opportunity to kill his brother, who fought for the other side.

Depending on who they wanted to requisition supplies from, some of the militia was known for switching sides regularly. Thus a number of battles of the American Revolution had less to do with any real political or military goals, but rather were vendettas or feuds, much like the Hatfields and McCoys of the late 19th century. At least one series of battles was fought over an unpaid gambling debt. Is it any surprise Patrick Ferguson considered many of these men to be little more than *"damned Banditti"*

Contrary to popular belief, many colonists preferred to sell their crops and other supplies to the Crown rather than Congress. Congress and its troops, when they bothered to pay at all, paid in Continental paper money. Continental money was commonly referred to as "shin plasters," as its only value was to bandage minor scrapes; it was worthless to the suppliers. Crown forces, on the other hand, paid with script redeemable in hard currency at varying distances based on how loyal to the Crown they thought you were. Loyalists might be able to redeem the script at regimental level commands at regional headquarters in New York, Philadelphia, Charleston, and Savannah. If you were uncooperative, you may have had to go back to London to redeem the script. Hessian troops were much preferred by merchants since they generally paid in hard currency (gold or silver coin) at the time of the purchase or requisition.

While the Battle of Brandywine was far from the only action Ferguson's Corps saw, it was certainly the most extensive. Sadly, Ferguson's wounds from the battle would end his Experimental Rifle Corps. A short time prior to Brandywine, Pattie's correspondence with Lord General Howe indicated that Howe was quite pleased with the success of Ferguson's Experimental Corps and was planning to double the number of men under Pattie's command. Regrettably, a musket ball destroyed his right elbow at Brandywine and cut these plans short. In his letters to his family he joked about his injuries from the musket ball, jesting about whether he or the worms would keep his arm.[29]

Some historical references list his troop losses at Brandywine at twenty-five percent, but this can be misleading, He was attached to a detachment of Queens Rangers under Capt. Wemyss, who took twenty-five percent casualties. Ferguson's Corps lists two killed and six wounded, including Ferguson himself. For what should have been a career-ending injury, Patrick would receive £187.10s King's Bounty for the effective loss of his arm. Though he returned to duty some months later in the Southern Campaign, it was only after a long recuperation on his part.

Some folks attribute the deployment of only forty-five men that day to equipment failure, and use it to support arguments in favor of the fragility of the Ferguson Ordnance Rifle's stock. Others misattribute the severe casualties taken by the Queens Rangers early in the battle to Ferguson's men. We would argue that the theory of the forty-five count being solely due to equipment failure is unsupported. If we assume a total of sixty-seven men (the number of rifles Ferguson says he had) removing forty-five would leave one section of fifteen men to guard and keep the camp. If we presume fewer than ninety (the highest number Ferguson uses to describe his unit), taking half the men into the field while leaving the other half as reserves is also a reasonable tactical approach. Since the era of Alexander the Great the normal rule of thumb is thirds: 1/3 committed, 1/3 reserve, 1/3 resting, while rotating your troops through those thirds. In other words, today's reserve is tomorrow's committed or primary force. Resting is now reserve and yesterday's committed troops are in a rest cycle. Of course the odd push may change this cycle, but committing 100% of your troops to anything means that you do not have reserves to pursue new opportunities, and that no one is fresh to keep the pressure on the enemy or to repel a counterattack.

The record shows that in skirmishes prior to Brandywine, Ferguson lost at least six men to enemy action. You can generally assume 10-15% of troops "not fit for duty" due to injury and/or illness. Therefore, there is any number of logical, tactical, and logistical reasons not to commit 100% of your force to any one action. In writing to his brother George after the Battle of Brandywine, Ferguson states:

To George Ferguson, [written between] 8 October 1777, Wilmington, Delaware - 21 January 1778, Philadelphia

My Lads were so fatigued with dashing after the Rebels over all Surfaces that I found it necessary to leave one half by turns in the rear with the column of march and work my way with the other - which as my whole detatchmend was under 90 men was no great command: however by avoiding the road, gaining their flanks, or keeping up a rattling fire from the ground or by bullying them we Still got on: - amongst other feats the troops behind us were witnesses when my 30 Lads advanced to a breast work of 100 yards in extent well lined with men Whose fire they received at twelve yards and when every body thought they were all destroy'd they Scrambled into the breast work and the Dogs ran away leaving even their Hatts and Shoes by the way:[30]

Ferguson typically wrote to his family about the failure of the artillery he had designed, losses to his command, and even his own injuries, so we would expect to see letters about the failure of any significant number of rifles. They were, after all, his "bairns." Patrick seemed to share his joys and challenges with his family, albeit slightly sugar-coating the bad.

On September 6th, 1777, he had taken twenty-four men into skirmishes against the Americans, but he reported forty-five men fielding five days later for Brandywine. This again brings up the theory that stock failure was possibly a significant factor that limited the amount of troops in the field. The stock is certainly a weak point in the design, and many surviving examples show damage in that area. However, to leap to its failure being a significant factor at Brandywine cannot be adequately supported.

There are authors who believe that all Ferguson's rifles were turned back into Crown stores immediately after the Battle of Brandywine. Luckily, correspondence from General Wilhelm von Knyphausen, overall commander of the Hessian troops, and the notes from the Army records are still extant. They do not sound like a return to stores order:

Head Quarters, 12th Sept 1777

Sir,
The Commander-in-Chief has received from Lieutenant-general Knyphausen the most honourable report of your gallant and spirited behavior in the engagement of the 11th, on which his Excellency has commanded me to express his acknowledgements to you, and to acquaint you, Sir that he shall, with Great satisfaction, adopt any plan that can be effected to keep you in the army under his command.

For the present, he has thought proper to incorporate the rifle corps into the light companies of the respective regiments. I am very happy to be even the channel of so honourable a testimony to your spirited conduct and of your late corps...

The following day, army records reflect:

HQ Camp on Heights of Brandywine. 13th Sept.

After Orders, Evening Gun firing, The British Riflemen are to join the Light Companies of the Regiments to which they respectively belong [31]

In our opinion this does not sound like a dismal failure. In fact, we interpret these orders to mean that the men returned to their respective Light Companies as riflemen, along with their accoutrements. At various points during the war, the 71st Regiment of Highland Foot had both replacements and regular troopers who were clad in a variety of garments and accessories, including green coats. These were due to re-supply issues and replacement men who were still wearing the uniforms of their old units when they were reassigned after recovering from illness or injury. Moreover, many retained the arms of their previous, and in some cases now defunct, units. Men used what they had until it was no longer serviceable.

There is an entry, dating from the spring of 1778, in the records of the Carlisle Peace Commission, stating:

> ....what mortified him (Ferguson) most was that during his confinement the rifle corps, deprived of their leader, was broken up,.....the rifles lodged in the store of spare arms [in the Artillery Park, Walnut Street, Philadelphia] and the men returned to their respective regiments [32]

However, we do not find Army records or journals that support that third party reference. Most modern scholars feel that oft-quoted citation was incorrect since the rifles were made use of during later actions in New York.

Note that the original plan of the experimental company was to return to their respective regiments. The correspondence from Knyphausen's staff indicates that this was, indeed, the case. There appears to be no malice on the part of the general staff. It was a reasonable expectation, given his injuries, that Patrick Ferguson would not be able to reassume command of his Experimental Rifle Corps. Additionally, there was little expectation he would ever take the field again with the probability of infection and death associated with battlefield medicine during the period.

20-21 Sept 1777 Battle of Paoli
British Officer 2d Light Infantry

We marched then briskly still silent - our Company
was advanced immediately preceeding a Company of

61

Riflemen who always are in front - a piquet fired at us
at the distance of 15 yards miraculously without
effect- this unfortunate Guard was instantly
dispatched by the Riflemens swords [33]

This excerpt would seem to strongly indicate that Ferguson's riflemen, with their sword bayonets, may have been the ones to silence the rebel sentry. This appears to refute the theory that Ferguson's rifles were sent into storage.

There is also an army order dated February 21, 1778, calling for reports of the number of rifles belonging to Ferguson's late corps which were now in the possession of other regiments.[34] Therefore, at least six months later, we know some were still in use. Again, this evidence seems to reprove the theory that Ferguson's rifles were sent to storage.

We disagree with some scholars interpreting the July 24, 1778 order as a "clean sweep" order. We feel the gang molds and armourers tools would also have been requested, as these components would require repair as well. However, the existence of the order clearly indicates they were still in the field almost a year later. On March 10, 1783, the General Return of Stores report from New York included seven Ferguson rifles that were unserviceable. If all of them were turned in at Philadelphia, how did they get to New York? [35] Were some sent to various central stores? If so, when and where?

Following the American Revolution, Patrick's family would continue to sell and manufacture Ferguson-type rifles, and these were used extensively by the East India Company both as militia and sporting arms. In fact, in 1797, General James McHenry and George Washington explored the idea of purchasing them as the new standard weapon for the new United States Army.[36]

Patrick Ferguson and the End of the Brandywine Campaign

The "Washington shot" at Brandywine in March of 1777

Whilest Knyphausen was forming the Line within a mile of the Rebell camp to wait for G Howes attack, their Rifle men were picking off our men very fast by random Shots from a wood some hundred yards in front as it is easy to do execution upon such large objects (I had only 20 men with me (a few having been disabled by the Enemy the rest from fatigue) who however proved Sufficient for my Lads first dislodged them from the skirts of the wood then drove them from a breastwork within it after which our purpose being answered we lay down at the further skirt of the wood not unnecessarily to provock an attack being so few without Support We had not layn long when a Rebell Officer remarkable by a Huzzar Dress passed towards our Army within 100 yards of my right flank, not perceiving us - he was followed by another dressed in dark green on blue mounted on a very good bay horse with a remarkable large high cocked hat I ordered three good shots to steal near them and fire at them but the idea disgusted me and I recalled them. The Huzzar in returning made a Circuit, but the other passed within 100 yards of us, upon which I advanced from the wood towards him; Upon my calling he stopd, but after looking at me proceeded. I again drew his attention and made signs to him to Stop, levelling my piece at him; but he slowly continued his way.[37]

Ferguson wrote that he and three of his sharpshooters were scouting the American lines near Chadd's Ford, along Brandywine Creek, (from which the name of the ensuing battle was derived), when they heard the approach of two horsemen. The first was a brilliantly clad Hussar and the second, a few paces behind, was wearing the traditional blue and buff uniform of an American senior officer, mounted on a bay horse and wearing *"a remarkably large cocked hat"*. He also noted that the Officer was of *"exceptional distinction"*. It is obvious that if Ferguson had indeed recognized General Washington he would have said so, and not taken the time to describe him as he did. It is also important to note that in the 18th century, there were few likenesses or images of people published, so Ferguson would have had to have met or at least seen Washington to have recognized him in this instance. The Hussar dress was most unusual in the American Revolution, with Kasimir Pulaski, a Polish Hussar who served with the Americans, being one of the few who wore it.

Ferguson's first thought was to cut the two riders down where they sat, so he ordered his men *"to steal near to them and fire at them."* Shortly thereafter, he changed his mind and signaled his men to hold their fire. He thought his first impulse was *"disgusting"*. Shooting officers so coolly going about their duties without warning felt like murder to Pattie. He stepped from his place of concealment and ordered the Hussar, the closer of the two, to step down from his mount. The Hussar shouted an alarm while his companion whirled his horse around and trotted off. Ferguson recorded the incident:

As I was with the distance, at which in the quickest firing, I could have lodged a half dozen balls in or about him before he was out of my reach, I had only to determine, but it was not pleasant to fire at the back of an unoffending individual who was acquitting himself coolly of his duty, and so I let him alone. The day after I had Just been telling this Story to some wounded Officers who lay in the same room with me, when one of our surgeons (who had been dressing the wounded Rebell Officers) came in and told us that they had been informing him that General Washington was all morning with the Light Troops generally in their front and only attended by a french Officer in a huzzar dress he himself mounted and dressed as above described; The oddness of their dress had puzzled me and made me take notice of it. I am not sorry that I did not know all the time who it was [38]

Of course, it turns out the tall colonial officer was General George Washington, most likely mounted on *Nelson*, his favorite horse. Captain Ferguson's sense of honor may have indirectly assured the colonial victory!

Ricky's Version of the Washington Shot: Battle Accuracy of the Ferguson Ordnance Rifle

The particulars of the event we are about to describe and Patrick Ferguson's demonstrations for King George III at Woolwich have both been decried by various historians as Crown propaganda and mere hyperbole, designed to frighten the American Rebels with reports of accurate shots and rates of fire that were impossible with 18th century arms. However, we were able to duplicate much of what has previously been called "impossible" with Ricky's Ferguson.

Our goal was to set up a range test designed to simulate a center mass, torso-sized target, so Ricky cut a thin piece of plywood 14 inches by 19 inches, an area that approximates the area of the chest and abdomen of most adult people. The wood was painted white and hung from a target frame at 100 yards at our home range. On March 9, 2010 at 8:45 a.m. Ricky started the test. Several older gentlemen were setting up beside Ricky, and they were interested in what he was trying to achieve. He explained the purpose of the test to them after grabbing half a dozen waxed balls and putting them into his pocket in preparation.

We set up to time Ricky's run, starting with the first shot and stopping after his seventh shot. He fired as fast and as SAFELY as he could while still aiming at the target 100 yards away. During regular demonstrations we have reached a rate of seven rounds fired in a minute, but this is razzle-dazzle, just a good show. Firing seven shots in a minute does not leave much time for aiming with any degree of accuracy at a target.

It took one minute and thirty seconds to fire these quickly-aimed shots. Although Patrick Ferguson could shoot six shots a minute in his demonstrations, this was a pure selling point for his prototype breech-loading rifle. In the field, Ferguson would only allow his men to fire three carefully-aimed shots a minute. The high-speed loading demonstrations were undertaken to illustrate that this new breech-loading rifle had a higher rate of fire than any other firearm at the time. In fact, until the metallic cartridge era, and the advent of lever action rifles, the Ferguson achieved the highest rate of fire of any firearm for almost 100 years. As you can see from the image below we can prove that Captain Ferguson could have lodged five or six balls in the tall colonial officer before he rode out of sight, although this is a moot point since only one sixty-two caliber ball blasting through his chest would likely render him unable to ride off the field.

Seven shots, 90 seconds offhand, at 100 yards with the Ferguson Rifle. Target is 14 x 19 inches and generally torso-sized.

When Ricky finished shooting at the target, he showed it to the gentleman who timed him. He replied "So… you got General Washington! Your trial begins next week!"

Why was Washington Not Worried?

Now why did the Hussar and the officer with "exceptional distinction" just turn about and ride away? Were they not afraid of Ferguson and his rifle? One explanation may be that at a distance of more than 50 feet it is rather hard to tell the difference between a Ferguson Ordnance Rifle and a more common Long or Short Land Pattern Musket (the Brown Bess).

The following series of images demonstrate what we mean:

Matt Morehouse and Ricky Roberts seen from 25 yards. One has a Long Land Bess, one a Ferguson Rifle. Which is which? (*Image courtesy of Uschi Van Ness*)

Matt Morehouse and Ricky Roberts at 50 feet. One has a Long Land Bess, one a Ferguson Rifle. Again, which is which? (*Image courtesy Uschi Van Ness*)

In addition, Ferguson's green uniforms looked quite similar to the Kings/Queens Rangers or the British Legion, all of which were predominantly armed with muskets and smoothbore carbines with a practical effective range of about 80 yards. Therefore, at a distance of approximately 100 yards, it is not very surprising that they rode off after obviously not sensing any particular risk in ignoring Pattie's order to dismount. However, if Pattie or his men had fired at such a close range it is not likely Washington or Pulaski would have had any chance of leaving that field alive.

Ricky Roberts in white with the Ferguson Ordnance Rifle and Matt Morehouse in Ranger Green with the Long Land Pattern Bess at 10 feet, a good comparison of a Long Land and Ferguson Rifle. Even with one next to the other the lines are similar. If compared to a shorter Light Infantry carbine they are even more closely matched. (*Image courtesy Uschi Van Ness*)

Steve Doyle and Ricky Roberts dressed in green. Which man has a Ferguson Rifle and who has the Light Infantry Carbine?

Patrick Ferguson and the Ferguson Ordnance Rifle at the Battle of Kings Mountain

Romanticized portrait of Patrick Ferguson. This was painted prior to the discovery of any period likenesses. (*Image courtesy Kings Mountain National Military Park*)

Throughout the month of December 1779, Patrick Ferguson did not allow his injuries to quell his drive or his love for military life. As hostilities expanded, with the French declaring war on the British, and Lord General Howe being sent to more strategically critical commands, Pattie lost little time reaching out to his successor, General Henry Clinton, in order to rejoin the fighting. Pattie was putting forward a plan whose purpose was to use provincial troops to expand the army regular troops who were being pulled back to more tactically sensitive areas.

The American Revolution was considered a nuisance at best, as the Americas were not yet profitable colonies. It was commonly anticipated in Britain that the colonists would be begging forgiveness and asking to return to the Crown within six months of declaring independence. Thus, moving regulars back to more vulnerable and profitable areas, replacing them with provincial troops, and training these provincial troops as light infantry made sense in the overall British plan at the time.

> *....an Army composed of 6000 regular foote and 6000 Light Infantry ....could act more decisively than one of twice its number that had fewer light Corps fit for Scrambling pursuit or detachment.....Light Infantry*

could act with Advantage in concert with the Line in an attack, in this irregular War, & would answer all other purposes. [39]

...it is only now become nessacery to exert a degree of Severity, which would not have been justifiable at beginning , when the Justice of the Claims of the Government were very doubtfull, as well as highly impolitic, whilst there was a probability of a friendly accommodation.......; but at present when the most ample Concessions are treated with the utmost insolent contempt, & when the Colonys persevere with the utmost inveteracy in their avow'd Design of assisting our heretofore natural & common Enemy to overwhelm the Parent State, the necessity of disabling an irreconcileable Enemy, that owes its Power to hurt us not only to our Protection & increasing fostering Care before the War, but even our foreberance since, will justify the Miserys that want of Nature & of Gratitude may render nessacery [40]

Pattie recognized the need to neutralize the French fleet and close the pirate and smuggling bases along the eastern seaboard, in the process protecting the crops and stores of known Loyalists. The British attempted to recruit all Loyalists, regardless of creed or color, including *"Indians from the back country,"*[41] since they were also threatened by the Rebels. This was because American settlers refused to abide by the 1763 Royal Proclamation Line that guaranteed all lands west of the Appalachian mountains to the loyal Indian allies after their support against the French in the Seven Years' or French and Indian War. Through various land companies Rebel leaders like George Washington, Benjamin Franklin, and John Adams were nonetheless making their fortunes while buying and selling land in contravention of Crown law.

Pattie was successful in bending General Clinton's ear and soon obtained a new command formed from regular troops of the 5th Regiment of Foot and the 3rd Battalion of New Jersey Loyalists, giving him a cadre to help train up the other provincial militias in light infantry tactics. He had already gained a name for himself as a soldier trained in *La Petite Guerre* (little war), a military concept which we now refer to as "guerilla warfare."

Pattie was brevetted as a lieutenant colonel in this role as inspector of militia. Brevetting signifies that he wore the rank and duties of a lieutenant colonel, but retained the pay grade of a captain. He used his troops to great effect at Chestnut Neck and Egg Harbor in New Jersey, the latter of which stirred up a bit of turmoil with Kasimir Pulaski, the Hussar he spared at Brandywine. Pattie became embroiled in a battle of broadsides and newspaper editorials in the *Rivington Royal Gazette* and other periodicals, debating the events of Egg Harbor, where Ferguson soundly defeated Pulaski by surprising his outposts, who had not been established correctly. After Ferguson successfully captured and destroyed rebel supplies there and routed the "rebel pirates" who were operating in the vicinity, Pulaski attempted to spin this defeat as "the Egg Harbor Massacre." (For a full discussion of this event refer to Appendix D)

Pattie took full advantage of the turmoil and public interest generated by these writings to engage in some psychological warfare with the rebellious colonists, deriding them the futility of their battles against the Crown and encouraging them to return to the English fold.

Having fully recovered from his wounds taken at Brandywine in 1777, in the spring of 1779 Pattie was in command of *"horse & foote & riflemen made up of a little of scraps & fragments that otherwise possibly might have been little employ'd"* [42]

Ferguson's successes in the New Jersey actions gained him the favor of General Clinton, who granted him a major's slot in the 71st Highland Regiment. As James Ferguson discusses in his book *Two Scottish Soldiers and a Jacobite Laird*:

> *Among the inhabitants of the Carolinas there were many loyalists or "Tories," for, in that State, large numbers of Scottish Highlanders had settled, and there, as in the Mohawk valley in the far North, the*

royal troops were certain of a friendly welcome from the Highland colonists. Argyllshire, Skye, and Ross and Sutherland in particular, had sent their surplus population in large numbers to the fertile lands of the Carolinas.........Possibly it was with some consideration for the feelings of a large number of those to whom he was now to appeal, that he was appointed Major of the 71st, a regiment raised in the Northern Highlands, from which many of these colonists had come. It was now proposed that " the well affected should be armed in their own defence," and he was entrusted with the duty of marshalling the militia over a large extent of country. In the proclamations he issued, in his new character of administrator, he called upon the people of South Carolina to restore the civil government of their country, under the favourable conditions then offered by the King and Parliament of Great Britain. A numerous militia was soon enrolled, who followed him " with the utmost spirit and confidence " ; they were allowed to name their own officers, with the reservation that, as they had also to act as civil magistrates, the authorities should be satisfied that the appointments were only given to fit and proper persons, who would not abuse their trust. " Ferguson," says Dr. Adam, " exercised his genius in devising a summary of the ordinary tactics for the use of this militia, and had them divided in every district into two classes,—one of the young men, the single and unmarried, who should be ready to join the king's troops to repel any enemy that might infest the province ; another, of the aged and heads of families, who should be ready to unite in defending their own townships, habitations, and farms. In his progress among them he soon gained on their confidence by the attention he paid to the interests of the well-affected, and by his humanity to the families of those who were in arms against him." [43]

That the battalion was technically only troops of wounded and invalids convalescing back in Britain or sitting in Patriot's hands in New England did not matter; it meant a promotion and a pay increase in a Royal regiment. With this major's role Pattie actually turned down the militia lieutenant colonel's pay he was technically entitled to once General Clinton officially appointed him to the office, feeling this sort of double dipping for the same job was improper behavior, although it was, sadly, a common practice.

[May 1780]

Sir Henry Clinton in December did me the honor of appointing me L^t. Col. by brevet in the Prov^l. forces & Since that Major 71st (as I was obliged by a new regulation to descend from the former) & I am now appointed to an office of neither rank nor Emolument, but which I am persuaded will prove usefull to our Country & of Course Creditable to me. It is the Charge of forming & disciplining the Militia here as Inspector. The inclosed hand Bill will show the Object of it. I could have 20 or 30 shillings a Day for it, but in fact I have a guinea already as major, so that it is no Sacrifice & a Decent act to refuse it, amidst the general greed for Plunder that is the bane of all the civil Department of this Army.[44]

Pattie continued in field command of Loyal American Volunteers registered on the rolls of the British Army as "Ferguson's Corps." He would lead, train, and use as cadre men assembled from remnants of the 5th Foot and the New York and New Jersey provincial militias (these included the Kings American Regiment, Loyal American Regiment, the Prince of Wales Regt, and the New Jersey Volunteers) in training other militia in the Carolinas for the remainder of his career. The corps was mustered at New York in the closing months of 1779, and officers and men prepared for the dangerous service, on which they were to sail, and on the 26th of December, 1779, sailed from New York, with the army under Sir

Henry Clinton, and after a dangerous voyage arrived at Savannah, Georgia.

The general muster on leaving New York, and which follows, includes the names of officers, non-commissioned officers, and privates, with the names of regiments and captains of companies from which they were transferred:

The American Volunteers

Major Patrick Ferguson, Seventy-first Highlanders, Commander. Captain Abraham DePeyster, King's American Regiment, Second in Command.

From the King's American Regiment.

Sergeant Asa Blakesly -	Captain Thomas Chapman's Co.
Drummer Francis Good -	Captain John Wm. Livingston's Co.
Pvt Jonah Cass -	Captain Thomas Chapman's Co.
Pvt David Jones -	Captain John Wm. Livingston's Co.
Pvt Samuel Carey -	Captain John Wm. Livingston's Co.
Pvt Silas Howe -	Captain John Wm. Livingston's Co.
Pvt Patrick Headon -	Colonel Edmund Fanning's Co.
Pvt Daniel Blue -	Lt-Col. George Campbell's Co.
Pvt Noah Pangborn -	Captain Isaac Atwood's Co.
Pvt Peter Simpson -	Captain Isaac Atwood's Co.
Pvt John Dalton -	Captain Robert Gray's Co.
Pvt David Fraser -	Major James Grant's Co.
Pvt Christopher Nicholls -	Major James Grant's Co.
Pvt William Miller -	Captain Abraham DePeyster's Co.

From the Loyal American Regiment.

Lieutenant Anthony Allaire.
Lieutenant Duncan Fletcher.

Sergeant David Ellison -	Captain Simon Kollock's Co.
Pvt John Fratingsburg -	Colonel Bev. Robinson's Co.
Pvt John Main -	Colonel Bev. Robinson's Co.

Pvt Samuel Sharp -	Colonel Bev. Robinson's Co.
Pvt James Campbell -	Captain William Fowler's Co.
Pvt John Strong -	Captain William Fowler's Co.
Pvt Thomas Donelson -	Lt.-Col. Bev. Robinson's Co.
Pvt Sylvanus Cronk -	Lt.-Col. Bev. Robinson's Co.
Pvt David Duff -	Lt.-Col. Bev. Robinson's Co.
Pvt Samuel Roan -	Captain Christopher Hatch's Co.
Pvt William Kemp -	Captain Christopher Hatch's Co.
Pvt Stephen Williams -	Captain Christopher Hatch's Co.
Pvt Francis Turner -	Captain Christopher Hatch's Co.
Pvt Stephen Chapple -	Captain Simon Kollock's Co.
Pvt Henry Smedgel -	Captain William Howison's Co.
Pvt Jordan Morris -	Captain William Howison's Co.
Pvt William Longstaff -	Captain William Howison's Co.
Pvt Ahamerus Terwilliger -	Major Thomas Barclay's Co.
Pvt Nathaniel Chambers -	Major Thomas Barclay's Co.

From the First New Jersey Battalion

Surgeon Uzal Johnson	
Captain John Taylor	
Sergeant John Campbell -	Captain Garrett Keating's Co.
Corporal John Evans -	Captain John Taylor's Co.
Corporal Samuel Hibber -	Captain John Cougle's Co.
Corporal Christopher Sheek -	Captain Joseph Crowell's Co.
Pvt Levi Hall -	Captain John Taylor's Co.
Pvt Peter Hawn -	Captain John Taylor's Co.
Pvt Ebenezer Darwin -	Captain John Taylor's Co.
Pvt Malaciah Bowham -	Captain John Taylor's Co.
Pvt John Hazen -	Captain John Cougle's Co.
Pvt Henry Mills -	Captain John Cougle's Co.
Pvt James Matthews -	Captain John Cougle's Co.
Pvt James Barclay -	Captain John Cougle's Co.
Pvt Eliagh Quick -	Captain Joseph Crowell's Co.
Pvt Robert Erwin -	Captain Joseph Crowell's Co.
Pvt Daniel McCoy -	Captain Joseph Crowell's Co.
Pvt Henry Berger -	Captain Joseph Crowell's Co.
Pvt Michael Miller -	Colonel Joseph Barton's Co.
Pvt Joel Daniels -	Colonel Joseph Barton's Co.

Pvt Joshua King -	Major Thomas Milledge's Co.
Pvt Clement Masters -	Major Thomas Millidge's Co.
Pvt Boltas Snider -	Major Thomas Millidge's Co.

From the Second New Jersey Battalion

Lieutenant William Stevenson.

Sergeant James Causlin -	Captain Norman McLeod's Co.
Corporal Randle Ensley -	Major John Antell's Co.
Pvt Henry Horn -	Captain Norman McLeod's Co.
Pvt Nicholas Myzin -	Major John Antill's Co.
Pvt Hugh Jones -	Captain Donald Campbell's Co.
Pvt Edward Donnelly -	Captain Donald Campbell's Co.
Pvt John North -	Captain Waldron Blaan's Co.
Pvt Conrad Kingstaff -	Captain Waldron Blaan's Co.
Pvt John Worth -	Captain Waldron Blaan's Co.
Pvt John Hurley -	Colonel John Morris' Co.
Pvt Mordecia Starkey -	Colonel John Morris' Co.

From the Fourth New Jersey Battalion

Captain Samuel Ryerson.
Lieutenant Martin Ryerson.

Sergeant Charles Brown -	Captain Samuel Ryerson's Co.
Sergeant Richard Terhune -	Colonel Abraham Van Buskirk's Co.
Corporal Thomas Mulvain -	Captain Samuel Ryerson's Co.
Corporal Ralph Burris -	Captain Samuel Ryerson's Co.
Pvt George Dickerson -	Captain Samuel Ryerson's Co.
Pvt Martin Wolohan -	Captain Samuel Ryerson's Co.
Pvt James Crab -	Captain Samuel Ryerson's Co.
Pvt John Troy -	Captain Samuel Ryerson's Co.
Pvt Ezekiel Pulsifer -	Captain Samuel Ryerson's Co.
Pvt Zopher Hull -	Captain Samuel Ryerson's Co.
Pvt Thomas Wilkins -	Captain Samuel Ryerson's Co.
Pvt William Vaughan -	Captain Samuel Ryerson's Co.
Pvt Walter Coppinger -	Colonel Abraham Van Buskirk's Co.
Pvt Robert Thompson -	Colonel Abraham Van Buskirk's Co.
Pvt John Hayes -	Colonel Abraham Van Buskirk's Co.
Pvt Joseph Westervelt -	Colonel Abraham Van Buskirk's Co.

Pvt Peter Spear -	Colonel Abraham Van Buskirk's Co.
Pvt Jacob Westervelt -	Colonel Abraham Van Buskirk's Co.
Pvt Joseph Pryor -	Colonel Abraham Van Buskirk's Co.
Pvt John Shetler -	Captain William Van-Allen's Co.
Pvt Caspaures Degraw -	Captain William Van-Allen's Co.
Pvt Sylvester Ferdon -	Captain William Van-Allen's Co.
Pvt William Van-Skiver -	Captain William Van-Allen's Co.
Pvt Benjamin Furman -	Captain William Van-Allen's Co.
Pvt David Dobson -	Captain William Van-Allen's Co.
Pvt John Crane -	Captain Philip Van Courtland's Co.
Pvt William Thompson -	Captain Phillip Van Courtland's Co.
Pvt Laurence Kerr -	Captain Phillip Van Courtland's Co.
Pvt Samuel Babcock -	Captain Phillip Van Courtland's Co.
Pvt Samuel Young -	Captain Phillip Van Courtland's Co.
Pvt Patrick McQuire, Snr. -	Captain Phillip Van Courtland's Co.
Pvt Noah Killohan -	Captain Samuel Ryerson's Co.

From DeLancey's Third Battalion

Sergeant Henry Townsend -	Captain Edward Allison's Co.
Sergeant James Cocks -	Captain Charles Hewlett's Co.
Pvt George Innis -	Captain Edward Allison's Co.
Pvt Gilbert Boodle -	Captain Edward Allison's Co.
Pvt John Gleoron -	Captain Edward Allison's Co.
Pvt Noah Gildersleeve -	Captain Edward Allison's Co.
Pvt Alexander Cain -	Captain Thomas Lester's Co.
Pvt Daniel Wanzer -	Captain Thomas Lester's Co.
Pvt Abraham Nichols -	Captain Thomas Lester's Co.
Pvt Frederick Cronckite -	Captain Thomas Lester's Co.
Pvt John Hevaland -	Captain Charles Hewlett's Co.
Pvt John Banack -	Captain Charles Hewlett's Co.
Pvt John Gibbs -	Captain Elijah Miles' Co.
Pvt Moses Olmstead -	Captain Elijah Miles' Co.
Pvt John Sherman -	Captain Elijah Miles' Co.
Pvt John Sharpe -	Captain Elijah Miles' Co.
Pvt Paul Wooster -	Captain Elijah Miles' Co.
Pvt George Weekly -	Captain Gerhardus Clowes' Co.

Summary

Surgeon	1
Captains	3
Lieutenants	4
Sergeants	8
Corporals	6
Drummer	1
Privates	100
Total Strength	123

Patrick Ferguson's second in command was Captain Abraham DePeyster, of the King's American regiment, a young scion of one of the old Dutch families of New York, whose family and descendants remain prominent in that state. He died in St. John in 1798, and sleeps in an unmarked grave in the Old Burying Ground in that city. Depeyster was an officer Pattie though very highly of and greatly desired for his command as seen in his letter to John Andre requesting DePeyster's transfer to his command.

Decr 11 1779

Dr. Sir

Captn. DePEYSTER of Fannings who I mentioned to you to Day, conceiving that as Eldest Captain of the Regiment the Choice of Serving in the <u>Volunteer</u> detacht from the Provincial Regiments would not be disputed with him, has not only put himself to the Expence of preparing for Embarkation, but as Colonel INNES & I had the same Idea, was desired to make the necessary arrangements for assembling & Quartering the different partys on Long Island; before he set out to wait on the Comd. Officer of the Regt which is 36 Miles distant.

The Captn. named by Major GRANT to go is by no means the first for Duty, & that being the Case, I cannot but hope still to have the Advantage of C. DePEYSTER's assistance on the Proposed Service; & that the General will not disapprove of his request.

Excuse this Trouble from Dr Sir   your most Obedt. H. Sert. Pat: FERGUSON

Unless you think that the above state of the Case favors Captn DePEYSTERs Claim, I beg that you will not mention it to his Excellency- but DePEYSTER would certainly be of use to the Detacht. [45]

The other officers were Captain John Taylor, of the First New Jersey Battalion, who was wounded during the campaign in South Carolina, at the close of the war he settled at Weymouth, Nova Scotia, where he died. Captain Samuel Ryerson and Lieutenant Joseph Ryerson, of the Fourth New Jersey Battalion, whose descendants became eminent in the Province of Ontario. The largest number of volunteers were from the Fourth New Jersey Battalion.

Lieutenant Anthony Allaire, of the Loyal American Regiment, born at New Rochelle, New York, of Huguenot descent, died at Fredericton, New Brunswick, and may be styled the historian of the corps. Lieutenant Duncan Fletcher, of the Loyal American Regiment, died at St. Andrews, New Brunswick. Lieutenant William Stevenson of the Second New Jersey Battalion, who died at Weymouth, Nova Scotia, with his friend and brother officer Captain Taylor.[46]

Now there is some debate as to the uniforms worn by Fergusons Corps. The units they from where they came were all in Green coats with black facings and white lace on the button holes for uniforms between 1778 and mid1780. And those Regiments went to Red coats with blue facings and while lace in mid 1780. So based on time some historians feel they may have been in Red Coats with blue facings (rather conflicting with the idea that Ferguson was the only Red Coat on Kings Mountain. He was the only Regular, but was he the only Red Coat?). However, Ferguson and his men separated from their parent commands 16 December of 1779 when they sailed from Lloyds Neck NJ for New York, and then shipped out for Savannah from New York 26 December 1779 with General Clinton arriving in Charleston February of 1780. So they were not in NY for the issue of new red coats in May-June 1780 and we have found no evidence of red coats ever being issues to them, so they very likely were still in green coats for the Southern Campaign. Add to this the confusion that occurred 0n Saturday, March 11th, 1780 when General Patterson's army crossed the Savannah River, and entered South Carolina without opposition. On March 14th the first mishap in the campaign occurred, and is given as recorded by Lieutenant Allaire:

> *Major Cochrane, with the British Legion, were in pursuit of a party of rebels, but, being mis-piloted, he arrived just before break of day in front of our picket. He immediately conjectured that we were the party he had been in pursuit of all night. He halted and made a position with an intent to attack as soon as it began to be clearly light; but the alertness of our sentinels obliged them to come on sooner than they intended. He immediately, on their firing, rushed on the picket; they gave the alarm, but were driven to the house, where our men, ready for the attack, expecting it was rebels, a smart skirmish ensued. The sad mistake was soon discovered, but not before two brave soldiers of the American Volunteers, and one of the Legion, were killed, and several on both sides badly wounded. Col. Ferguson got wounded on the arm by a bayonet.*[47]

The authors find this confusion easier to explain if Ferguson's Corps is wearing something other than red coats. You have to be, pretty close together to bayonet someone dark green and dark blue both go to black in the dark, and red would be harder to confuse.

Ferguson led his men with skill and vigor in the Carolinas and maintained his staunch opposition to the plunder and abuse of the colonists. After the fall of Charleston, General Clinton offered a general pardon to any colonists not in the Congressional Army if they would cease taking up arms against the king, swear an oath to the same, and return to their homes and farms. This clemency was not extended to those known to have murdered loyal citizens or who remained bearing arms against their king.

> He possessed," says General de Peyster," many of the qualities which ennoble a soldier. He was temperate in his habits, magnanimous in his disposition, fearless in danger, and manly at all times. Such was the confidence reposed in him by Cornwallis that he conferred on him a brevet of Lieutenant-Colonel; constituted him a local or territorial Brigadier-General of militia; confided to him an independent command, and allowed him to select his own subordinates and troops."
>
> "Colonel Ferguson possessed qualities peculiarly adapted to win the attachment of the marksmen of South Carolina. To a corps of originally 150, but soon reduced by disease and hardship to 100 picked men, Provincial regulars {i.e. seasoned volunteers from New York and neighbouring States), armed with his rifles, he soon succeeded in attaching about 1300 or more hardy natives, until, as he advanced, his command increased to 2000 men, besides a small squadron of horse.[48]

Pattie continued to recruit new troops to the Loyalist militias by guaranteeing their terms and area of service. He also issued "*ammunition and oznabrass* [oznaberg was a linen blend fabric] *for a rifle shirt*"[49] Pattie continued to go to great lengths to prevent predation by the colonists:

> You will pay particular attention to restrain the militia from offering violence to innocent and inoffensive people, and by all means in your power to protect the aged, the infirm, the women and children of every denomination from insult and outrage.[50]

A plug bayonet inserted into muzzle

On May 31, 1780, Ferguson drew from stores captured from the Patriot forces at Charleston, South Carolina *"300 serviceable French Muskets and bayonets and 50 sea service swords."* [51] These arms were probably for the militia troops Ferguson was helping to bring together and train. Interestingly, he also had plug bayonets with wooden handles to match the bore made up by the blacksmith for those men without "modern" socket bayonets. However, his adjutant, Lieutenant Anthony Allaire, did not know what to call them, and described them as long daggers with iron guards and handles turned to fit the muzzle. While they certainly existed and were used at various points in the American Revolution, this could not be used as an argument for plug bayonets being common in the Southern campaigns.

Waxhaws

On June 1, 1780, Pattie received word of Banastre Tarleton's victory over Colonel Abraham Buford at the Waxhaws, where Tarleton offered generous terms of surrender. Buford's men were to be paroled to their homes and allowed to retain their arms, while their officers were taken back to Charleston. The terms were refused by Buford, who stated that they would *"defend* [his position] *to the last extremity."* To make matters worse, some of Buford's men opened fire while the surrender parley was still in place, a serious breach of military etiquette. Buford fled his poor decision and ill chosen words, abandoning his men to his poor choice. Nevertheless, Rebel propagandists twisted this into a tale of *"cruel treachery"* and *"brutal slaughter,"* while making *"Remember the Waxhaws"* and *"Buford's Quarter"* battle cries of the force of rebellion. Later, at Kings Mountain, Patrick Ferguson

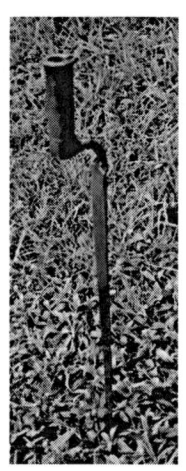

Light Infantry Carbine Socket Bayonet.

and his men would suffer dearly for this propaganda.

Nothing in the historical record indicates that the British Legion was "brutal" or there would not have been as many prisoners after a refusal of quarter at the Waxhaws. Is being attacked on foot by mounted dragoons scary as hell and prone to exaggeration from the foot troops? Absolutely, but that does not make it any different from any other foot soldiers "taking horse." Either you are well disciplined and hold, and can "repel horse," or you fail, your ranks are broken and you are "defeated in detail with sword and bayonet." Taking the bad end of a cavalry charge is a lot like being tossed down a steep hill into a dumpster full of rocks and an angry bear.

We have to keep in mind that Tarleton's horse was shot out from under him during the parley. Even after Buford refused surrender terms, the American white flag was still raised when the shot was fired, killing his horse and plunging Tarleton to the ground, looking very much as if he had been shot dead. This is supported by the journal of American surgeon Robert Brownfield, who was part of Buford's command. Breaking the rules of war tended to be a sore spot for British troops who were strictly bound by them, and suffered dearly for the rebels' abuses of them. Legion troops who, even by Tarleton's description, engaged in "*a vindictive asperity not easily restrained*" with approximately 350-380 soldiers under Buford's command. Of these men, 203 were captured, and admittedly 150 were so badly wounded they were left behind, attended by surgeons from both sides. However, it was hardly a massacre to the last man, as propagandists would have you believe, and Tarleton did not even secure the nickname "Bloody Ban" until Robert D. Bass's 1952 book *The Green Dragoon*. After the American Revolution, Tarleton became a politician, dividing much of his time between the army and Parliament, as supported by his journals.

Propagandists fashioned Tarleton and Ferguson into "boogeymen," with little grounds for doing so on either count. This is similar to British accounts of American Francis Marion, known as the "Swamp Fox", who is often credited with three or four atrocities a night, sometimes hundreds of miles apart, or the comparable horrific exploits that Americans attributed to Simon Girty on the western front of the war.

Approach to Kings Mountain

On the way across the Carolinas en route to Kings Mountain, Pattie paroled a prisoner, Samuel Philips, to carry a message to the Back Water Men (Over Mountain Men) supposedly warning them *"if they did not desist from opposition to the British arms, he would march his army over the mountains, hang their leaders, and lay their country waste with fire and sword."* As this message was verbal (it is somewhat odd that a professional soldier such as Ferguson would not have written the message instead of relying on the sometimes faulty memory of another) and the only sources of it are the Rebels, there is some question as to its authenticity, and many historians attribute it to one of several rebel firebrands and propagandists.[52] Some even attribute it to the agitator Reverend Samuel Doak, a Princeton-trained minister who made frequent use of the expression "fire and sword" in his sermons, in an effort to stir up the rebellion within his parishioners. Doak was a protégé of John Witherspoon and a fervent opponent of David Hume (author of *A Treatise on Human Nature*), the Scottish Enlightenment, and the English Crown. His congregations were primarily Ulster Protestants who viewed the Revolution as a Calvinist holy war.[53] The Georgia and the Carolinas colonies had been under a state of intermittent war since the 1750s as part of the Presbyterian Rebellions. It really makes little sense, with the advantage of retrospect, to send a verbal message since the officers and clergy that he was sending the communiqué to certainly could read and, more then likely, the courier delivering the message could not. Regardless, Pattie was caught up in a maelstrom of trouble that would end his days and cost his command dearly.

The comments of Capt. Johann Ewald, commander of the 2nd Company Hesse Kassel Jäger Korps, about the beginnings of Ferguson's militia command shows he thought little of these men:

> *In the afternoon some sixty loyal inhabitants arrived from the mountains demanding officers, arms, and ammunition to serve the King and take revenge on*

their neighbors, who had oppressed them very much up to now. They asserted that a great number of their comrades had already gone over to Lord Cornwallis.- I do not trust these people, for what can such a handful of men undertake? I believe they are carrying out a deception to obtain arms and ammunition and to use them against us. It is said that Major Ferguson has volunteered to lead these people.[54]

In addition, this raises interesting questions as to whether Ferguson was baited into the role he would play on Kings Mountain.

" His orders were," says Washington Irving, "to skirr the mountain country between the Catawba and the Yadkin, harass the Whigs, inspirit the Tories, and embody the militia under the royal banner. He had been chosen for this military tour as being calculated to gain friends by his conciliating disposition and manners; and his address to the people of the country was in that spirit :' We come not to make war upon women and children, but to give them money and relieve their distresses.'" From other sources we learn that he added/' he hoped they would excuse him if, meeting with their husbands or brothers in the field, he should use them a little more roughly." "Ferguson, however," says the American author," had a loyal hatred of Whigs, and to his standard flocked many rancorous Tories, besides outlaws and other desperadoes ; so that, with all his conciliating intentions, his progress through the country was marked by many exasperating excesses."[55]

It is fascinating to explore the idea that Patrick Ferguson was planning to cross the mountains, as was purported in the "message" he supposedly sent across. He had no orders from Cornwallis or Clinton to do so; his orders were to form and train a militia for operations in the Carolinas. Admittedly, at this time, those "over the mountain" areas which are now Tennessee were part of North or

South Carolina, but he only had 100 experienced troops forming the core of his command, and the balance of his command was green as grass, since they were brand new militia conscripts. This is hardly a command you would want to take over the mountains to battle the enemy in their hearth and home, with no dragoons or artillery. Most of these men were in the first 60 days of their militia duty, and could barely march, let alone fight.

The Crown forces were not permitted to live off the land and seize foodstuffs and material from the local Loyalist inhabitants. Food had to be either purchased, or requisitioned from the quartermaster. Most of it was shipped in from Great Britain, although undoubtedly some was seized from forfeited Rebel property. Ferguson's command, when captured, had no major food stocks for a protracted campaign over the mountains.

Washington County, Virginia, militiaman Benjamin Sharp Recount of the Over Mountain Men's Campaign:

During the whole of this expedition, except a few days at the outset, I neither tasted bread nor salt, and this was the case with nearly every man; when we could get meat, which was but seldom, we had to roast and eat it without either: sometimes we got a few potatoes, but our standing and principal rations were ears of corn, scorched in the fire or eaten raw. Such was the price paid by the men of the Revolution for our Independence. [56]

After Pattie's death at Kings Mountain his adjutant, Lieutenant Anthony Alliare, reported:

The morning after the action we were marched sixteen miles, previous to which orders were given by the Rebel Col. Campbell (whom the command devolved on) that should they be attacked on their march, they were to fire on, and destroy their prisoners.

The party was kept marching two days without any kind of provisions. The officers' baggage, on the third day's march, was all divided among the Rebel officers.

On the morning of the fifteenth...During this day's march the men were obliged to give thirty-five Continental dollars for a single ear of Indian corn, and forty for a drink of water, they not being allowed to drink when fording a river; in short, the whole of the Rebels' conduct from the surrender of the party into their hands is incredible to relate.

Several of the militia that were worn out with fatigue, and not being able to keep up, were cut down, and trodden to death in the mire.[57]

There is no evidence that Pattie had the resources needed (food, engineering tools, ammunition, and similar provisions) for a protracted campaign across the mountains. Add to that the utter lack of mounted troops, such as dragoons, or any artillery attached to his command, and it really calls into question as to whether or not Pattie was really headed over the mountains.

This broadside, which we can demonstrate came from Pattie, strengthens our position that the campaign was more of a call to defense than an expedition across the mountains:

Denard's Ford, Broad River,
Tryon County, October 1, 1780

Gentlemen:—Unless you wish to be eat up by an inundation of barbarians, who have begun by murdering an unarmed son before the aged father, and afterwards lopped off his arms, and who by their

*shocking cruelties and irregularities, give the best
proof of their cowardice and want of discipline; I say,
if you wish to be pinioned, robbed, and murdered,
and see your wives and daughters, in four days,
abused by the dregs of mankind—in short, if you wish
or deserve to live, and bear the name of men, grasp
your arms in a moment and run to camp.*

*The Back Water men have crossed the mountains;
McDowell, Hampton, Shelby and Cleveland are at
their head, so that you know what you have to depend
upon. If you choose to be degraded forever and ever
by a set of mongrels, say so at once, and let your
women turn their backs upon you, and look out for
real men to protect them.*

PAT. FERGUSON, Major 71st Regiment.[58]

The Revolutionary War pension application of Aaron
Deveny, Jr. tells the story of his capture near Gilbert Town, North
Carolina by Patrick Ferguson and his subsequent rescue by his wife,
who pleaded and cried for Ferguson to parole her husband. Ferguson
granted the parole, reportedly saying that he "would rather see 20
men dead than one woman in tears."[59] Deveny reportedly did not
join the other men paroled at Gilbert Town when they took off after
Ferguson with the Over Mountain Men; he stayed behind and
guarded the fort against the Indians. Mrs. Deveny was "sorry when
she heard of the death of Ferguson as he had treated her so
kind"[60].This is hardly what one would expect from a man crossing
the mountain with fire and sword.[61]

In addition, none of Ferguson's officers: Abraham de
Peyster, Alexander Chesney, Uzal Johnson nor Anthony Allaire,
made any comments in their respective journals about plans or
preparations for a campaign over the mountain. As these men
comprised his second in command and were division commanders,
one would think that they might have had an inkling of any such
plans. Whether or not Pattie proposed to do this, he would bear the
consequences of the perception that he may have sent such a threat.

Moreover, the flood of fury from the Over Mountain Men and the Carolina militias surrounding him was going to reach a climax at Kings Mountain.

Kings Mountain October 6th, 1780:

I arrived today at Kings Mountain and have taken a post where I do not think I can be forced by a stronger enemy than that against us.
I have wrote for the militia assembling under Colonel Floyd to join me tomorrow evening if not destined for another service.
I understand that we have little or no reinforcement to expect from Colonel Cruger or his militia immediately. Good soldiers as reserves behind our riflemen and few real Dragoons to second with effect and support the Horse Militia upon the Enemy's flanks would enable us to act decisively and vigorously...[62]

Pattie made several requests for reinforcements, but Tarleton was recovering from yellow fever, and the other officers simply refused to comply, citing various excuses and maladies. The Over Mountain Men and Carolina militias flanked Pattie and his troops, so they could not make it to Cornwallis' position in Charlotte. Ferguson recognized his difficult position, but he was in as good a defensible position as possible given the resources and personnel he had available. In addition, the approaching Over Mountain Men were flanking his command. This denied him the time to put up even the most basic of defenses, so he had to rely on the terrain and the valor of his soldiers. Ferguson, recognizing the challenge of his situation, wrote in a note to Major Timpany of the New Jersey Volunteers:

Between you & I there has been an inundation of Barbarians, rather larger than expected...I should [not] *have thought myself justifiable in committing myself, had I not expected reinforcements*[63]

There were only enough Loyalist troops to form a single line around the mountaintop, since the Over Mountain Men had sufficient numbers to surround them and to maintain pressure on all sides.

A body of 600 men indeed, under Major Gibbs, were assembled four miles from the Americans at Cowpens, and on the morning of the 7th were only fifteen or twenty miles from Ferguson. Had they joined him, as it was expected they would in the course of the day, or had they marched to the firing, and fallen on the Americans while still held in check by the gallantry of the Provincials, the battle would undoubtedly have had a different ending. By so little did his last resource miscarry![64]

Pattie and his troops vigorously defended it, thrice driving the rebels back at bayonet point, but as the ammunition of the North Carolina Loyalist militia began to run low they fell back, leaving the 70 Loyal American Volunteers to bear the brunt of the oncoming Back Water Men.

A 2006 National Park Service archeological survey of Kings Mountain recovered 50 unfired and 81 fired projectiles ranging from .30 caliber through .70 caliber with .49-.52 caliber and .60-.62 caliber being the most commonly occurring.[65] Based on this information, it seems that most of the Back Water Men were armed with rifles in the .50 caliber range. The sub-.40 caliber balls in the study are attributed to pistols, but the authors feel these are actually rifle ball or shot for buck and ball loads. Eighteenth century pistols did not tend to use these sub-.45 caliber barrels; however, some small game hunting rifles do make use of them.

Interestingly, the larger caliber ball, the sole .70-caliber ball, dropped well behind the Patriot lines where their horses were being held.

Having driven back the Americans at the point of the bayonet, they poured a rifle volley after them; and "slowly and with great precision retreated, loading their rifles as they retraced their steps, as they had learnt very skilfully to do by the example and instructions of Ferguson.[66]

DePeyster reported that after repelling the Back Water Men from the mountaintop, Ferguson's Corps was "reduced to twenty rifles."[67] At this point, Ferguson and the militia officers, Plummer and Husbands, led a last desperate attempt to break the enemy lines. A horrific volley struck them, killing Husbands immediately and seriously wounding Plummer. Pattie, conspicuous in his checked duster, bent right arm and sword in his left, sat atop his grey horse and rallied his troops. Rebel rifleman James Collins recalled, in his autobiography

...almost 50 rifles must have been leveled at him at the same time. Seven balls passed through his body, both his arms were broken, and his hair and clothing were literally shot to piece. [68]

The Loyalist wounded were abandoned by their captors to die on the mountain without surgeons or care of any kind. Though local Loyalists rescued some, most became carrion. People living in the region around Kings Mountain avoided eating hogs for some time after the battle since many of these hogs had feasted on the remains of the fallen. (Hogs in the period were commonly allowed to roam free for forage and then rounded up periodically, similar to the cattle round ups of the "Wild West" in the 19th century).

An additional seven hundred men, including the walking wounded, were captured. They were marched off the mountain by their American captors, each carrying several firelocks with flints or cocks removed (some sources say the Loyalists removed the cocks to prevent the Americans from using the firelocks). Along the way thirty men put on "trial" in a drum head court martial for crimes against Congress were sentenced to death. Most were saved; however ten men, including a man who attempted to escape, were hung. Ferguson's Corps Surgeon, Dr. Uzal Johnson, was assaulted for trying to treat a Loyalist prisoner for a sword cut suffered on the march.

Rebel troop strength	900-3200 (the number varies widely according to the source); 1000-1500 is most widely accepted.	
Loyalist troop strength	1075	
Rebel casualties	28 dead	64 wounded
Loyalists causalities	157 dead	163 wounded

Tarleton had recovered enough from his bout of yellow fever to command troops and artillery to support Ferguson's Corps by October 8th, but it was too late. He learned at Smiths Ford that "*every insult and indignity*" had been inflicted on Ferguson's body.

Patrick Ferguson remains at Kings Mountain, buried there by his aide and red-haired "Virginia Sal", one of the Loyalist women killed while treating wounded troops. Perhaps targeted because of her red hair, she and "Virginia Pol" (Pauline) were reportedly companions of Pattie. Some Victorian authors used this to paint an image of a wanton man; nevertheless, even if their hedonistic portrayal is true, it would not have gone against the grain of acceptable behavior for the time, especially given Patrick's social standing. Virginia Pol survived the battle, eventually made it back to the protection of the Crown, and supposedly became the companion of another British Officer.

After the Crown defeat at Kings Mountain, Pattie's legacy lived on. So respected was his training of these men by both sides that some of his surviving officers after Kings Mountain were offered pardons by Rebel commanders if only they would spend a month training their troops to the Light Infantry drill and tactics used by Patrick Ferguson. Every one of them refused the offer.

Modern Perception of the War and Kings Mountain

A number of authors attribute the British loss at Kings Mountain to the smoothbore Brown Bess, and musket balls actually

ROLLING out of the smoothbore barrels because they were aimed downhill.

How can we put this politely? That is absolute and unmitigated balderdash. Period ball was not a smooth, unblemished sphere like our contemporary ball bearing; they had a sprue (nipple-like nub) sticking out on them that was left over from casting and cutting off the gate. If you have ever accidentally dry-balled a musket (loaded ball without powder) then you know how vexing it is to pull that ball out without a modern 21st century carbon dioxide ball discharger. With a period-style ball puller, it takes between 15-45 minutes to extract a ball and often requires more than one person. Musket balls will NEVER, NEVER, EVER just roll out of the barrel, no matter how badly you may want them to.

Nonetheless, the fact that the soldiers were shooting downhill was absolutely a factor. Men shooting downhill generally tend to shoot high, just as those shooting up hill tend to shoot low. However, to reiterate, musket balls do not just roll out of a barrel. EVER!

The militia Patrick Ferguson was raising and training were armed with captured French muskets from the fall of Charleston, not Brown Besses. Though *some* of Ferguson's men *may* have been equipped with Brown Bess muskets, as purported by some sources, the archeological and documentary evidence shows that carbines (.62 caliber) of one type or another were more likely, as Ferguson drew no musket powder, ball or flints from the quartermaster in Charleston for his Corps. According to the journal entries of Allaire and de Peyster, about half of the men carried rifles (also .62 caliber). The only Brown Bess-sized ball (.69-.73 caliber, dropped or fired) recovered in the 2006 National Park Service archeological dig was a dropped ball from the Over Mountain Men camp, where people were left guarding their horses. None were found in the areas controlled by the Crown. It is an odd quirk of history that the only Brown Bess at Kings Mountain may not have fired a shot, and was in the hands of the American Rebel forces. The Loyalist North Carolina militias fighting for the British Crown had the French muskets generally associated with the American forces serving under George Washington.

It is the consensus of many historians that Ferguson's Ordnance Rifle did not make it to Kings Mountain. However, several historical inconsistencies have us digging deeper into the question:

1. When picking up supplies in Charleston, Ferguson ordered the British standard carbine ball (.615) and Double Glazed Rifle powder for his troops. Some historians say this is because Ferguson's Corps of Loyalist Troops had been issued 1776/1777 Tower Rifles. However, these rifles tended to be assigned to the regular light infantry company, while militia and Provincials were allocated the cast-offs and captured arms. There is no record of Ferguson having drawn any Tower Rifles for his command, and, since Ferguson "owned" his Experimental Company rifles, might he not have taken them along instead of going deeper into debt to obtain new Tower Rifles for his troops? In addition, the counts from the inspection returns indicate captured French musket for the militia and rifles for part of his Loyal Americans Volunteers Company, also known as Ferguson's Corps.[69]

2. Arent de Peyster reported that after repelling the Back Water Men from the mountaintop for the third time, Ferguson's Corps was "reduced to twenty rifles."[70] Other information indicates that they used bayonets to repel the Back Water Men. Arguably, this can be interpreted to suggest that bayonet-mounted rifles may have been part of the force driving them back. Only two rifles in the American Revolution mounted bayonets: Ansbacher Jaeger Rifles (all the Ansbacher Jaegers were in Canada at this time) and the Ferguson Ordnance Rifle.

3. Campbell and Shelby both reported rifles in the 1,500 stands of arms captured at Kings Mountain by the Over Mountain Men.

4. Campbell kept some stands of arms for his use and recompense, but turned over stands of muskets to Congressional forces.

5. Archaeologists and historians have been searching for .645 or .648 ball with the "wings" cut by the rifling as evidence of Ferguson Rifles. This is not correct. They shoot .615 ball and have a distinctive "kiss" of the rifling on the bare and unpatched ball it fires. We explore this in greater detail in other chapters.

6. We know Ferguson's second in command, DePeyster, had his breech-loading Ferguson Rifle with him at Wilmington, North Carolina after leaving New York.

7. James Collins of the Over Mountain Men wrote in his journal that "Ferguson was coming on with his Boasted Marksmen." This indicates that Ferguson had some kind of riflemen with him, and that they had a solid reputation for being sharpshooters.

8. All the Ferguson Ordnance Rifles known to exist today in the United States have one thing in common. They are war booty taken "back north" by Union troops after the American Civil War. If all the Ferguson Rifles were returned to the depot in Philadelphia, Pennsylvania, which is not exactly the Deep South, how were they captured somewhere in the Southern United States and taken back to the North in the 1860s?

9. The cock recovered by the 2006 archeological survey of Kings Mountain could be either a 1776/1777 pattern rifle or a Ferguson Ordnance Rifle. The authors believe this cock is from a Ferguson Ordnance Rifle—take a look at the images and see what you think.

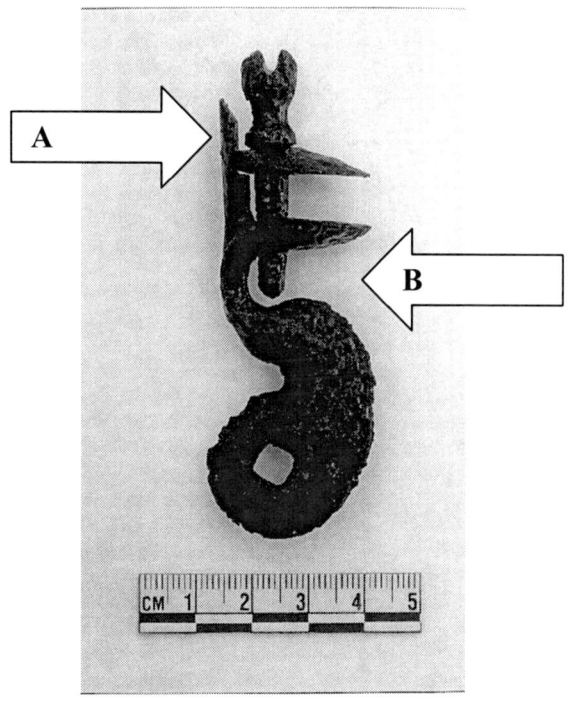

Cock recovered Kings Mountain 2006 - SEAC Cat # 2972

(Image courtesy Kings Mountain National Military Park)

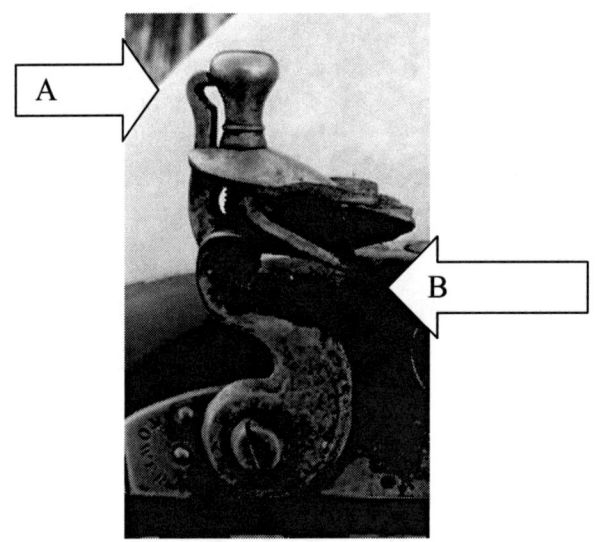

Cock on reproduction Ferguson

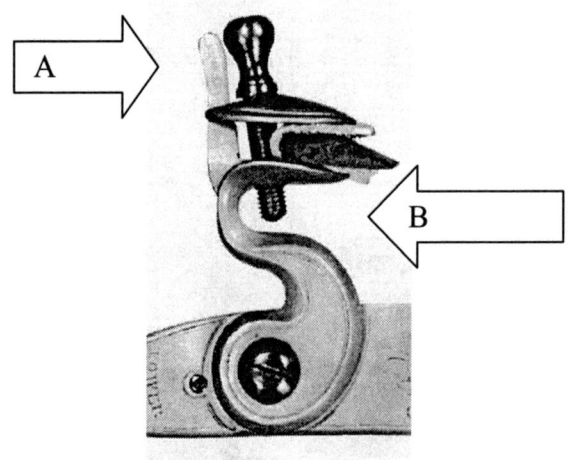

Tower 1776 Rifle reproduction
(Image courtesy of The Rifle Shoppe, Inc.)

Some historians suggest that Ferguson's riflemen at Kings Mountain had Tower Pattern 1776/1777 rifles, based on Ferguson's requisitions of carbine ball and rifle powder.

There are some objections to this view:

- The cock that was recovered from the Crown camp is clearly not a 1776/1777 rifle; to the authors, it appears to be a cock from a Ferguson Ordnance Rifle .

- Note that the jaw screw on the Ferguson and the recovered cock are pointed. The Tower is flat-bottomed.

- The Tower lock has a screw slot and hole. The hole is large enough that it would be impossible to take a sideways picture of the screw without seeing the edges of the hole; the hole through it is for a pin to tighten the jaws onto the flint. Both the dug example and the Ferguson cock have turn screw (screwdriver) slots.

- To the left of the turn screw on the recovered cock, the sharp angle just below the top is missing. When you look at the reproduction Ferguson cock and the recovered cock this is clearly visible. This angle seems to be exclusive to the Ferguson rifle cock.

We have also asked a couple dozen other period arms historians to review this same evidence. Ninety-six percent (96%) agreed that it is a Ferguson Ordnance Rifle cock, while three percent (3%) thought it was a Tower Rifle Cock. Another one percent (1%) said the recovered example was not a match to either arm. We'll leave it to the readers to come up with their own conclusion.

The authors believe this constitutes physical evidence that the Ferguson Breech Loading Ordnance Rifles WERE on Kings

Mountain! Never before has this been demonstrably proven by any historians, and you saw and read it here first! Do we expect debate on this conclusion? Absolutely, however, such debate fosters new findings, and this leads to a better understanding of history.

Morristown National Historical Park Original Ferguson Rifle

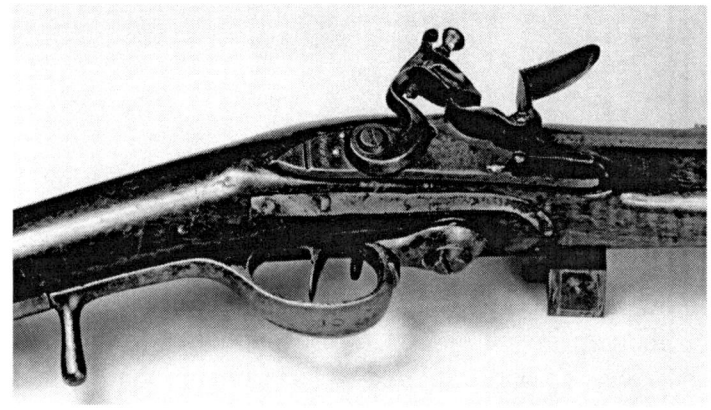

Original Ferguson Ordnance Rifle

(Image courtesy Morristown National Historical Park)

Original Ferguson Ordnance Rifle

Note this example has a Brass/Bronze breech versus steel. It is unclear if this is original to the rifle and exhibits a variation in the pattern, or if it is a replacement for a lost steel breech. (*Image courtesy Morristown National Historical Park*)

Milwaukee Museum Original Ferguson Ordnance Rifle

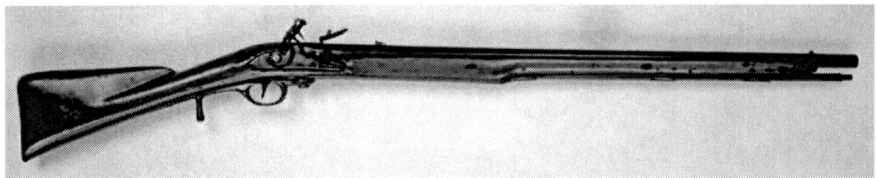

Ferguson Ordnance Rifle - Milwaukee Public Museum

(Image courtesy of Milwaukee Public Museum)

Now, are we proposing that Patrick Ferguson may have died carrying his own invention at Kings Mountain? No, not at all. His right elbow was so badly injured at Brandywine that he had to use his sword in his left hand while keeping his horse's reins in his teeth. He also had to teach himself to write and dress with his left hand (he even wrote a friend of how challenging the privy was with the buttons on period breeches. For the 18th century fashion conscious this would also indicate Pattie wore fashionable French fly breeches rather than common broadfalls). Add to that the still-healing bayonet wound he had in the left arm from an unfortunate friendly fire (bayoneting) incident with the British Legion in March of 1780 (when one night near Charles Town, South Carolina (today's Charleston) a nervous Legion sentry bayoneted him in the left arm). Pattie was a driven and very talented man, but we doubt that, given these infirmities, even he could have managed to fire his rifle one-handed. Frankly, we are amazed at the determination of the man to maintain a command in the field.

There are enough inconsistencies to whet our appetites to keep researching the question of exactly how far to the south the Ferguson Ordnance Rifle served during the Revolution. Moreover, did it serve with Ferguson's Corps at Kings Mountain? We believe we have answered that question with a resounding "yes". Where does the evidence take you?

Care and Feeding of the Ferguson Ordnance Rifle

Dress for Shooting the Ferguson

Isn't that just the coolest picture?

The hat Ricky is wearing in the above photograph is a striped railroad hat. Now, in spite of recent fashion trends, that backwards hat is not a fashion statement! You will notice the hat has a solid back with no open space for the snap. Ricky uses this to keep the heat off of his forehead. He later found out that the only practical purpose for an 18th century cocked hat (commonly called a tricorn) is to deflect the heat off your head. You really do not want a wide brim

Ricky's first Powder flask for the Ferguson

hat to catch the heat that blows out of that breech. We have since learned that a wider brim can be used if it is pulled down close to your eyebrows as long as the brim does not extend to the rotating breech, but a shorter brimmed hat is recommended. With the rotating breech at the rear of the Ferguson Ordnance rifle, you get a bit of gas coming out of the rifle when you fire. The heat will not burn enough to injure you but it is HOT and distracting.

Most of the time when we are demonstrating the Ferguson Ordnance Rifle we are in proper 18th century period attire; however, none of the photographs that we have in proper costume are nearly as good! This is Ricky in his native costume, West Carolina Farm Boy. If he were not shooting the Ferguson, his hat most certainly would not be on backwards!

All of the flame that you see above is coming from a full chamber of @65 grains European Match Grade 3F powder propelling a .615 lubed ball down a barrel measuring .648 across the grooves (deepest part of the rifling) and .612 across the lands (shallowest part of the rifling).

Notice the orange cone of fire erupting out of the muzzle. The Ferguson shoots a nominally "undersized" ball, so the gas actually jets out around the ball before it exits the barrel. This may even help to clear fouling from earlier shots by blowing it out in front of the next ball. This is an untested hypothesis at this point; we would need fancier cameras to better test the theory. The Ferguson has very deep grooves with the ball just barely riding on the lands. This provides a place for the fouling to gather. As a result, Ricky has repeatedly shot his Ferguson forty-eight rounds without fouling up the bore or the action. Round forty-eight is just as accurate as round one. Why forty-eight rounds? For some reason, we kept ending up at the range with forty-eight balls.

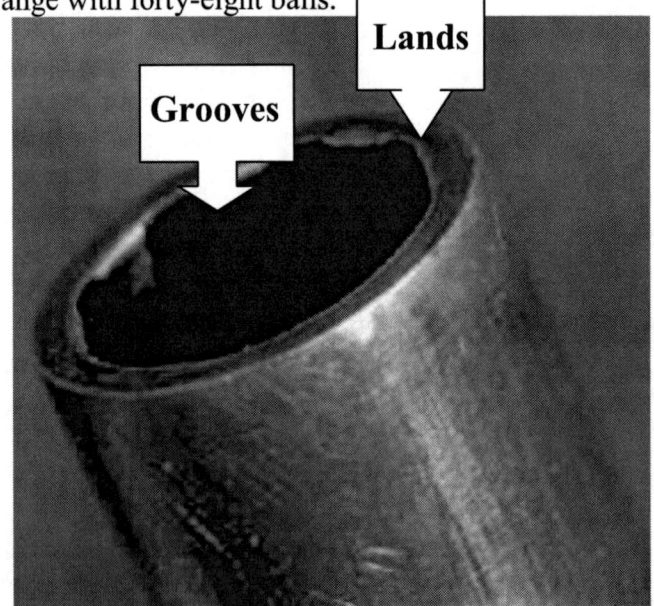

Muzzle of Ferguson Rifle showing lands and grooves.

Ricky's Ferguson Ordnance rifle is a low number Narragansett (#085). In some black powder shooting circles a few folks have said that the earlier Narragansett rifles had shorter powder chambers than the later ones, while others say that earlier ones had larger chambers. Based on measurements from the chambers on a later Narragansett Ferguson #214 (and Bryan's Ferguson that he later built from The Rifle Shoppe, Inc. parts) also having a @65 grain chamber, we are fairly certain that the chamber volume was not altered during production, and therefore there is no need to buy more than one in search of the mythical larger chamber. Note: sadly, Narragansett Arms is no longer in business.

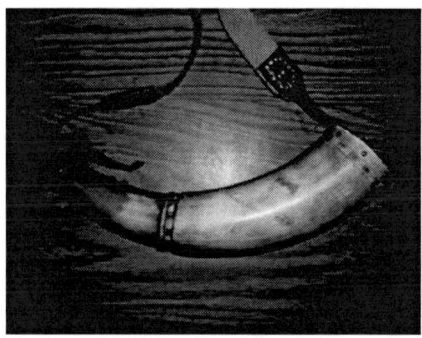

Ricky's "Seneca run horn" used for speed demonstrations.

Above you can see the powder flask Ricky made for the rifle. The Ferguson rifle has a tapered powder chamber so you cannot overload it.

Xavier Della Gatta "The Battle of Paoli" (*Image courtesy of The American Revolution Center*)

The big question with operating the Ferguson Rifle is the 'how' of the loading of the powder. We have some documentation on the uniform color of Ferguson's Riflemen, and we know that powder flasks were ordered before Ferguson and his Corps left Britain, but we do not know for certain what they looked like. Nor do we have clear evidence they were ever actually delivered to Ferguson. The above 1782 painting by Xavier Del Gatta entitled *The Battle of Paoli* depicting the battle on September 20, 1777 shows a

small group of Ferguson's riflemen possibly wearing powder horns (common for Light Infantry). However, no cartridge boxes are visible—neither belly (common for Light Infantry) or shoulder/battalion boxes. Moreover, the British Army in this period commonly loaded from paper cartridges. As far as concrete shooting and loading information is concerned, Ferguson left none—only hints and nibbles!

Matt Morehouse Kings Rangers   **Jim Van Ness Hesse Kassel Jaeger Korps**

Sketch of Uniform of Fergusons Rifle Corps based on Del Gatta. (Author drawing)

1. Light Infantry hat cocked on one side.
2. Epaulets to retain straps, madder red
3. Woolen Infantry Coat Green Powder Horn on strap (note the straps on Ferguson's men are much narrower than the cartridge box straps on the Highlanders in the foreground.
4. Powder Horn
5. Cuffs that can be rolled down as mittens.
6. Ferguson Sword Bayonet on buff leather cross belt.
7. Weskit Green (we cannot see it in the picture but we assume they are Light Infantry Weskits with slash pockets on the breasts for ball and flint.)
8. Gaitered trousers brown (Gaitered trousers are long pants [in an era of knee breeches] that are loose in the thigh and rump but snug in the calf and cover the shoe top and keep out stones, etc. and generally a strap going under the shoe to keep them from riding up the leg.)

So now we continue our work with the other records and some experimental archeology. For those of you not familiar with the concept of experimental archeology, it is a process whereby one tests their interpretation of historical records with real world tests to determine the validity of a hypothesis. Some hypotheses get supported and some do not, and sometimes we come up with a new hypothesis based on what we have learned. Who says history is boring? This stuff is infectiously good fun.

Are you paying attention? Ricky and the Ferguson Rifle sword bayonet

Loading and Firing the Ferguson Ordnance Rifle

Firing the Ferguson rifle

Ricky has been shooting and competing with long rifles and other muzzle-loading arms for over thirty years. He tried to load his Ferguson rifle on his first trip to the range as he would with any long rifle, using a powder horn and a separate powder measure. Now, unless you are an octopus or maybe a squid, this is impossible to do with a Ferguson breech loader. You need to hold the rifle with your left hand and access the powder with your right. Paper cartridges work well in this situation, but the hanging powder measure on your rifleman's bag does not. To solve this problem, Ricky crafted a wooden powder flask similar to the European military flasks of the previous century. It uses a spring-loaded valve. You can document this type of valve and measure setup for other period flasks.

We know Ferguson ordered flasks but we do not have any descriptions or patterns to copy. Frankly, we cannot even confirm that he ever received any of them. Although no verifiable patterns have yet been identified, it is quite possible that his men made do with "light infantry powder horns," another item mentioned in historical records of the period.

This now brings up a safety issue. We will be going directly to the rifle with a flask spout. This is a severe NO-NO in the world of modern muzzle loading. There is a risk of a spark or hot spot remaining in the bore of the long muzzle loader barrel that might ignite the dropped powder charge. If poured directly from a horn, this should probably be prefaced with "Hey y'all watch this."

Because the powder does not go in first, the Ferguson Rifle is not a muzzleloader. A greasy ball is loaded into the breech end, followed by the little finger of your right hand. Then, the powder goes into the chamber. After shooting our muzzle-loading firelocks many times at reenactments, we can burn our hand on the heat of the barrel, a barrel that can steam if water hits it. In our combined decades of living history and battle reenactment experience, never have we seen a firelock cook off under these conditions. For those readers that are not black powder aficionados, a *cook off* is an accidental premature ignition of the powder from sparks or embers in the barrel from a previous shot, or from built up heat in the barrel. This is more a concern with muzzle-loading artillery pieces than with muzzle-loading shoulder arms. Because the Ferguson rifle chamber is open at both ends, we are confident there is no lingering ember spark to set off the powder. As a result, we have no problem dumping powder behind the ball in this tube open at both ends. Of course, some of the locales where Ricky competes, such as the NMLRA shoots in Friendship, Indiana, require paper cartridges for loading because of safety concerns. This works well, but tends to take slightly longer than loading from the horn. We'll continue to explain the loading process assuming that you are using a horn.

Step 1: Half cock, open breech and insert ball. If you point the muzzle down, gravity generally seats the ball for you.

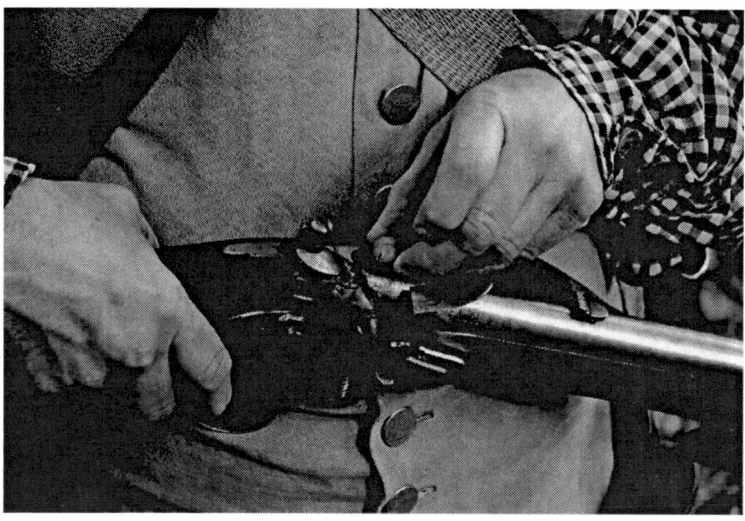

Step 2: If needed, you can make sure the ball is seated with your God-given Ferguson Ordnance Rifle Loading Optimization Tool, that is your right pinky finger. Generally, you only need to do this after 30-40 rounds, unless your balls are wax dipped, too thick or "nubby" from touching together while cooling.

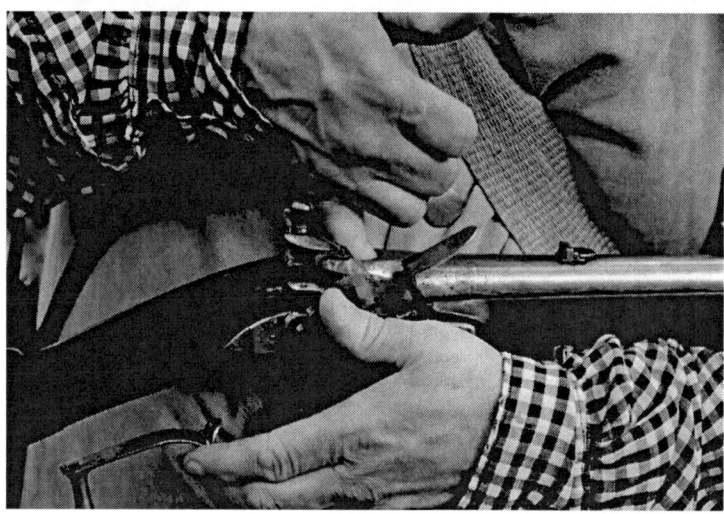

Step 3: Charge chamber with powder (3F black powder). A 65-70 grain measure tube or pre-measured paper cartridge makes this process faster and easier.

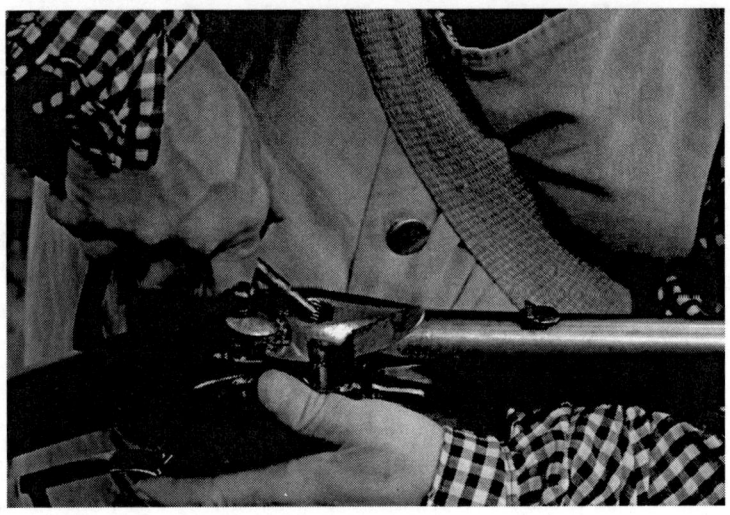

Step 4: Close breech, cutting out excess powder.

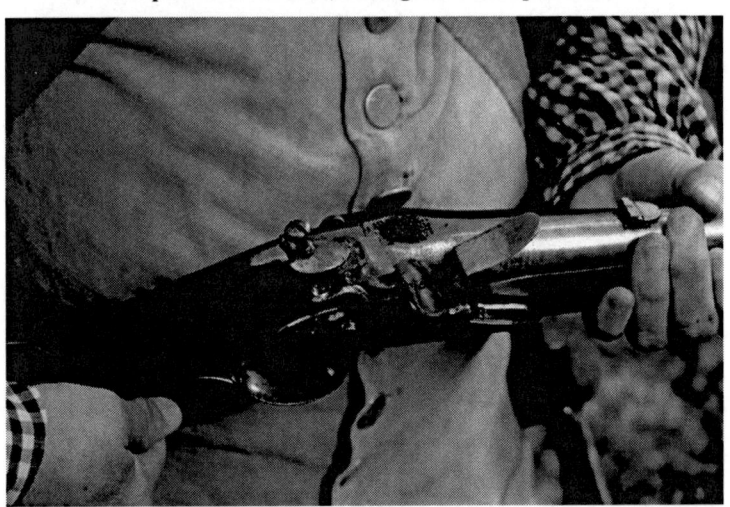

Step 5: Sweep excess into pan for priming, then shut pan. The Ferguson shoots a bit cleaner with less leakage if you measure the powder either via tube on the horn or via paper cartridges, and then prime separately. Nevertheless, this fill-and-sweep works just fine.

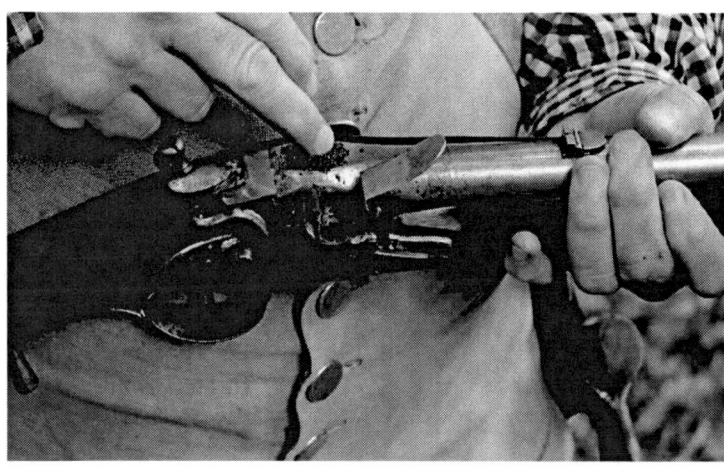

Take aim, go to full, cock and fire.

The method of priming that Ricky generally prefers is to put the powder in the pan before pouring the powder into the chamber. This ensures that you have prime in the pan. While trying to speed load this rifle, we both have on occasion raked the excess powder off too vigorously and missed the pan completely. Both methods work; it is simply a matter of preference.

Hmmmm…six steps to load and fire versus thirty-five steps in the 1764 Manual of Arms for a British musket. Let's be fair here. If we count the steps as meticulously as the Manual of Arms, there would be eleven steps for the Ferguson rifle, versus seventeen steps for the Brown Bess musket, as long as we limit ourselves to firing steps. This should definitely be placed in the plus column for the Ferguson Ordnance Rifle.

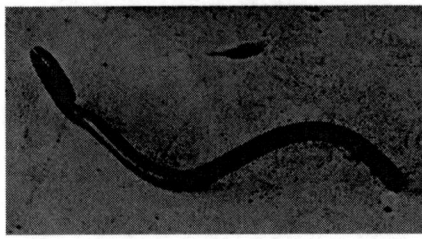

Ferguson Loading Tool

We experimented briefly with a "Ferguson loading tool" early on in the process, based on discussion with other Ferguson aficionados. However, we discovered that even a couple of ham-handed fellows like us had no trouble with using our right pinky on the occasions it was needed to help seat the ball. We never had to use the special ball-seating tool Ricky fabricated after purchasing his rifle. There is no evidence Pattie or any of his men used a tool like this and, based on our testing, there is no need for one. Pinkies work just fine. We wear the ring of black powder residue like a badge of honor. You can tell a Ferguson shooter by his Fergi-finger.

Lubing the Breech

If you just drop a ball into the breech, pour powder in behind it, and fire without any lubrication at all, you will have a one or two shot bayonet platform. This has been a common complaint of many who thought they could just pick up a Ferguson and shoot it. To be honest, it is a justifiable complaint in the all-steel breeched Ferguson Ordnance Rifle. There had to be some 18th century period lubricant used to grease the threads to keep the action moving. The identification of this lubricant took us some time and a bit of research to decipher.

There is an oft-referred "quote" in black powder circles referring to Patrick Ferguson scrounging around the British camp prior to the Battle of Brandywine for all of the tallow he could get his hands on. He purportedly made a pest of himself "hoarding tallow," and an officer mentioned it in his reports. Normally, we would not put forward an undocumented quote but the idea can be supported in a number of other ways. Tallow and beeswax are commonly used as components in period rifle lube throughout a variety of rifles and rifle cultures. In addition, the British sealed and lubricated their musket cartridges with mutton tallow. So, even without a firmly documented quotation, we felt it a valid path for experimentation. Our goal was to make our Ferguson Ordnance Rifles operate as closely as possible to the way they did in 1776. Since there were so many ingredients and ratios, it just took some time before we discovered the right combination of beeswax and tallow. This gave Ricky an excuse to run to the range two or three times a week to test new lubrication ideas. Of course, anything that requires a range trip is a worthwhile endeavor!

Tallow is the hard, white top layer that results after rendering animal fat. Melt, filter, cool, and then repeat to render the fat down and separate the tallow from the grease for a better result. To get even purer (harder and whiter) tallow, you need to collect several batches and re-render them. Period folks may be interested in knowing that the Fergi-Lube formula we've had the most success with is the same as the tallow candles in common use during the 18th and 19th centuries.

Thick tallow sticks to the threads too firmly and gums up the works. Using too thick or too much lube creates issues with clogging the anti-fouling cuts and/or the "touch hole" (in quotes because it is largely a half-open cone in the rotating breech). Thin tallow blows out of the threads after four or five shots.

We have not found a manmade 20th century grease or oil that works properly. None. Trust us; we have pretty much tried every one of them! Candle hard tallow works well, but we had consistency problems after rendering with deer tallow (coincidentally, we later discovered deer tallow also makes poor candles). Most of the time deer tallow renders too soft and blows out of the threads. We have been told beef or mutton make the best candle tallow, but in time Ricky was able to come up with a non-tallow solution that we now use the majority of the time. Is it 100% period correct? No, but it will get us to at least sixty-two rounds. If you want 100% period correct go with mutton tallow.

The hot lubrication can hit you in the face and forehead, so it is very important to wear your hat or a headscarf and eye protection when shooting the Ferguson.

Fergi-Lube Recipe

Two parts beeswax
One part all-vegetable shortening

Melt the beeswax in the top of a *double* boiler (very important!) and after stirring in the shortening until it is melted and blended, let the mixture stand until firm. Only make as much as you can use in a year. As it ages, it becomes firmer and seasoned like a candle or soap and does not work quite as well. Old-time carpenters kept a plug of beeswax with them to apply to the threads of screws. They went in much easier lubricated with the beeswax.

Greased Ferguson breech

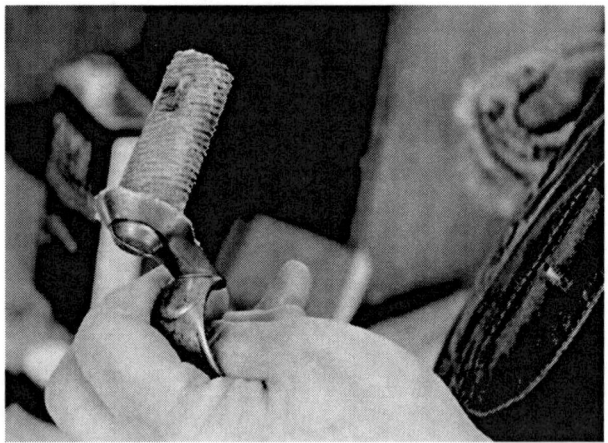

Ferguson breech showing anti-fouling cuts

It took Ricky a couple of months and one minor fire in his kitchen to come up with this particular Fergi-Lube formula.

- First he tried beeswax by itself, but this was too hard. At less than 30 degrees Fahrenheit it will stiffen so much you will start out with a no shot bayonet platform!

- The Fergi-lube mixture works well even when it is above 97 degrees Fahrenheit, since it does not loosen up to a great degree. Some folks in colder climes than the Carolinas report having good success with a 50/50 beeswax/vegetable shortening mix for temperatures below freezing. Therefore, you may need to tweak the recipe based on your season or climate. 2:1 works year round here in the Carolinas; your mileage may vary.

- We nearly forgot the important part! Melt the Fergi-Lube in a small cup and dip your cleaned breech threads in the wax. We usually prop the breech, top side down, on a paper plate or slab of clean wood if it is an outdoor event. Rubbing the hot metal (heated from the boiling water) with the lube will work well enough, but you will have to wipe the breech plugs at around 35-45 rounds and reapply the lube. We have found that dipping the breech into the lube has gotten us to 62 rounds so far, without any failures due to fouling and without the need to reapply lube.

Another field technique we have used with success, depending on the hardness of the candle, is to take a candle stub and rake it across the threads of the breech plug to fill the breech threads. This provides a quick, no melting, and fire method of waxing the breech. With some candle stubs we have gotten around 20-25 shots before the breech needs rewaxing. It all depends on the composition of the candle; we have taken a candle stub that we thought would work to the range and only gotten 8-10 shots off before we had to rewax.

Lubing the Ball

The story is not over yet. When Ricky went to the range with the tallow and proper .615 ball, the bore would foul up after only a few shots and the accuracy would quickly go down the tubes. Mind you, in 1776 Patrick Ferguson shot close to 50 rounds in his famous demonstration for King George III at Woolwich with no variation in accuracy.

Before the work was over, Ricky started thinking about back in the day when he loaded lead bullets in his handgun cartridges, when the lead bullets always had a grease ring or two to keep the bore slick and avoid rapid lead fouling. In addition, Bryan knew the German Jaegers carried a bit of wax and tallow in their ball bag to lube up the balls as they carried them. You cannot run naked lead balls down a rifled barrel without grease of some kind. Therefore, the next time Ricky melted the tallow for the breech, he took a pair of tweezers and dipped the .615 balls in the tallow mixture.

When he went back to the range the next time, with his newly tallowed breech and ball, his Ferguson rifle became the 1776 assault rifle just like Ferguson's rifle was way back then! That is when the fun started. We have also dipped the balls in pure bee's wax, which works just as nicely if it is very warm out.

In the next section, we will discuss the most vexing aspect of the Ferguson rifle—cleaning!

Cleaning the Ferguson

Well folks, we have mentioned the features we like most about the Ferguson rifle—the rate of fire, accuracy and the lack of fouling—so just to be fair, we will now show you the warts.

After Ricky had the shooting part figured out, he then needed to figure out how to clean the dang thing afterwards! Nearly all the shine goes off the penny when you get to this stage. Black powder, lead and tallow combine for some of the nastiest fouling you will ever see in a firearm.

Approach One: Modern Solvents and Patches

When Ricky got his Ferguson home, he got on the Internet and typed in "Ferguson Rifle," hoping to find some clever cleaning solution. One fellow said to clean it using about 100 solvent-soaked patches, which would take about 45 minutes of hard work. He was dead right about the patches and elbow grease. As a result, for the next two months Ricky tested different cleaning methods.

After testing all kinds of vile chemical concoctions, he got the time down to 20 minutes and 50 patches. But he knew there had to be a better way, since they did not have all our high-tech cleaners in the 18th century, and there was no way could Ricky imagine a whole company of riflemen using this method.

Approach Two: Tepid Water and Modern Cleaning Solutions

During two months of testing, Ricky tried cold water, tepid water, glass cleaner, and all variety of soaps, including dish soaps and detergents. He even tried a mix we call "whale oil," which is equal parts rubbing alcohol, hydrogen peroxide, oil soap, and furniture cleaner. Based on some quotes from other troops who claimed to have cleaned firelocks with urine, we even explored some "urine analogs" in weak ammonia and lye solutions. No pun intended, but…no soap. None of the above worked well for cleaning the Ferguson rifle.

Approach Three: Boiling Water

 There had to be a better way. Ricky was at King's Mountain National Park with Bryan doing their Ferguson demonstration and lecture when Bryan came up with the idea of using boiling water. Bryan regularly uses this approach with all his firelocks. Ricky had used water before, but not at a boiling hot temperature.

A Sparkling Clean Ferguson Rifle in Fifteen Minutes and Four Patches

The Ferguson Rifle's barrel is held in place by captive barrel wedges. It is easy to remove the barrel but you do need to take extra care with the stock. Take out the single lock screw, the tang screw and the forward sling mount screw. Stop. At that point you will run into another problem. When you take the barrel out of a muzzleloader, you generally just grab the muzzle and lift it out of the stock. If you do this with a Ferguson, you will split the stock in two because the breech runs all the way through the rifle. The best way to remove the Ferguson's barrel is to sit down and turn the rifle upside down with the barrel resting on your knee. Gently tap the breech with a wooden mallet and the barrel will fall out of the stock and onto your lap.

We have tried many different techniques of applying very hot water to the Ferguson. The following method is the best one we have found to date.

You will need the following items:

1. A bracket or notch where you can prop the barrel while pouring in the hot water. As you end up pouring the water down the muzzle, we have stuck the tang in the ground to help steady the barrel.

2. A leather glove or rag to protect your hand. The barrel will be much too hot to touch with your bare hands.

3. A nylon bristle brush for the breech cavity. A baby bottle cleaning brush works well.

4. A cleaning rod, two patches wet with cleaning solution and two dry patches.

5. Your favorite gun oil.

6. One half gallon of freshly boiled water.

Step 1. Pour the hot water on the breech plug and lock. Then, hold the barrel horizontally and pour a small amount of hot water through the breech cavity.

Step 2. Run the bristle brush through the breech cavity a few times.

Step 3. Pour a little water back through the breech cavity, then stand the barrel muzzle up in your notch or bracket and pour the remainder of the water down the barrel.

Step 4. While avoiding touching the hot barrel with you bare hands, run one solvent soaked cleaning patch down the barrel. It should come out close to clean.

Step 5. Run down the second solvent patch,

which should come out spotless.

Step 6. Run one dry patch down the bore, reverse it, and run it back down.

Step 7. Soak one patch in your favorite gun oil and run it down the still hot barrel.

Step 8. Using a leather glove or rag to pick up the barrel and lay it down horizontally, then use a ½ inch dowel rod and push the oiled patch into the breech cavity, "screwing" the patch in from the bottom end until it comes out of the top.

The inside of the barrel and breech is now clean. Use the second oil patch to oil the outside of the barrel and then set the barrel back in the stock. Most of the time, it is still too hot to touch with your bare hands. Be sure when you pour in the hot water that you are in a place where the very hot black crud can run without staining floors or tents or roasting your toes.

Now you will want to set the breech and lock on another flat board (a split log works fine for this), and pour the boiling hot water on them. You then have to level the barrel and pour down the breech. The lock cleans right up, and the barrel will be good, but you still have to wire brush the screw breech itself and run tight patches through the breech to get the gunk out of there. A few solvent-soaked patches will clean the barrel now.

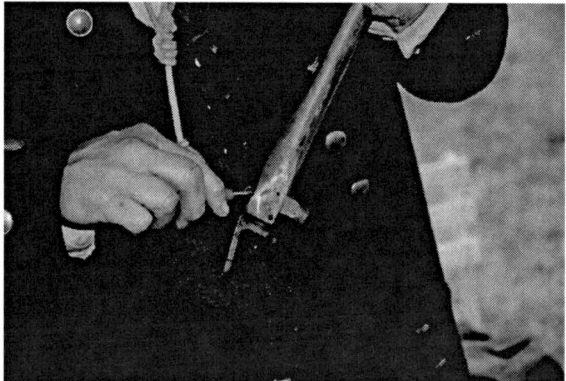

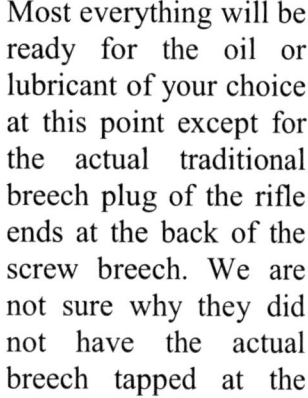

Most everything will be ready for the oil or lubricant of your choice at this point except for the actual traditional breech plug of the rifle ends at the back of the screw breech. We are not sure why they did not have the actual breech tapped at the same time they tapped the screw breech threads. Perhaps as a reservoir for the crud that failed to burn? However, the actual breech is flat kind of in a shallow hole. You will need to have a small 45-degree tool to clean this area because it is subject to draw rust!

Now we can clean the Ferguson in 15 minutes with about 15 patches. To reassemble the rifle, the barrel can be easily lowered into the stock while the rifle is right side up. While in the field at a historical event, there should be no problem finding a campfire to boil water. At the range, you may want a camp stove or a thermos of hot water for cleaning. One final note, the hotter the water is the better it works. Using lukewarm water will use up a box of patches and 45 minutes!

The 18th century method of hot water works far better than any other method we have tested. We are not talking about this technique as a be-all, end-all for any and all fouling from all black powder arms. However, when specifically cleaning the wax and grease lube mixture used in the Ferguson and some other period arms, it is by far the best option. Cleaning with water, especially boiling water, is something of a hot topic among modern black powder shooters. Some endorse the idea, while others are rather vitriolic in their opposition. One thing to keep in mind is that the British Army used boiling water to clean their arms well past the World War II era. They even issued special kettles and funnels for pouring the water down the bore when cleaning the SMLE rifle in their barracks. The British also included instructions for hot water cleaning in their manual for the Whitworth Rifle in the 1860's.[71] During World War II the United States, in the first issue of "cleaning solvent" we are aware of, was when it was supplied for the M1 Garand rifles. Prior to this water or urine was used for cleaning. The much vaunted GI corrosive primer cleaning solution was also water-based; that is why it could dissolve the caustic salts left behind by corrosive primers.

Photos of Ricky's Ferguson: Does the breech wear out?

With over 6,000 total shots fired, Ricky's Ferguson rifle has likely been fired rather more than any original model. (around 4000 shots when these pictures were taken) As we previously mentioned, Ricky's weapon is a Ferguson Ordnance Rifle by Narragansett, #85.

Ferguson Rifle with breech closed

The screw breech is attached to the trigger guard. One full turn of the trigger guard opens the breech.

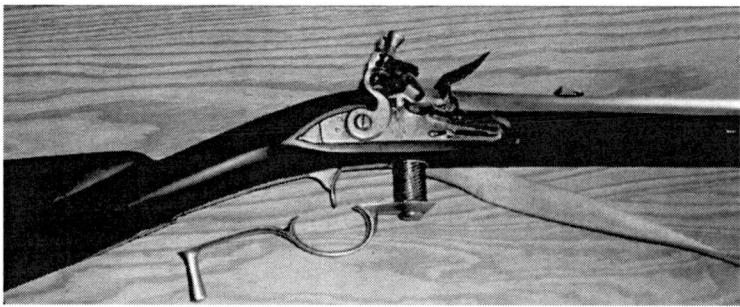

A close-up image of the screw breech showing Patrick Ferguson's 1776 patented anti-fouling grooves

Now sometimes you will see or hear when people start spouting the old wives' tales about the Ferguson Rifle. Falderal about it locking up, or the breech wearing out quickly etc.; in all our research and shooting our Ferguson Rifles, we have duplicated everything Patrick Ferguson did with his famous rifle test at Woolrich in front of King George in 1776. To date we have fired well over three thousand live rounds and at least that many demo balls for national and city parks where we can't shoot lead ball from Ricky's Ferguson Rifle.. To date on Ricky's rifle have worn out the frizzen (hammer in 18th century speak) to the point where it had to be recased twice and finally half soled due to wear. Late 2011 Bryan and Ricky had to install a touch hole liner in Ricky's rifle as all the shooting had blown out the touch hole. The only other sign of wear on the rifle is the wood forward of the screw breech on the bottom of the rifle. As many times as the trigger guard has been cranked open, the bearing forward edge of the breech is wearing on the wood. There is no additional wear on the screw breech threads the screw breech is as tight on Ricky's with over 6000 rounds fired as Bryan's with fewer than 500 rounds fired.

Fouling and the Ferguson Ordnance Rifle

Breaking the 48-Ball Barrier

Bryan shooting the very first live ball from his Ferguson

The authors took their Ferguson Ordnance Rifles to a local shooting range in March of 2009. The goal of this trip was for Ricky to break his old record of 48 shots. It has taken some time to try to do this, not because of any failure of the rifle, but because of the fact that we just keep ending up with only 48 prepared balls at the range. We originally used this number as a testing target since this is the number of shots reportedly fired by Patrick Ferguson for his demonstration for King George III at Woolwich. Once we successfully tackled the Fergi-Lube formula and ball lube process, we had little trouble meeting this 48 shot target repeatedly. For testing purposes, we shot on multiple occasions, with multiple Ferguson Ordnance Rifles, in various weather conditions across a period of several years.

From Ricky's journal—March 7, 2009:

I did an 18th century torture test. I did not fire these rounds super fast. As in an 18th century battle there would be no cleaning whatsoever. Firing slowly perhaps one round a minute of aimed fire the barrel started heating up after 8 rounds. Shots 9 & 10 were shot through a sea of heat waves. After shooting 10 rounds, I set the rifle aside for the barrel to cool.

After cooling, I shot 10 more. I brought another muzzleloader to shoot during the cooling periods. I brought 53-greased ball this time. I actually hollered when I shot # 49! I shot all 53 of my rounds when Bryan offered me some of his greased rounds. I shot seven of Bryan's rounds and took the total up to 60! A little later, when Bryan was shooting his Ferguson off a bench rest in an attempt to determine the sight picture. Bryan loaded and fired two more rounds out of Ricky's to see the difference between the two sight pictures. This brings the total up to 62 rounds fired. After round # 55, the action began to stiffen up some from the fouling. Nevertheless, we were still able to crank the action closed into battery. An outstanding day at the range! We stopped at 62 rounds because we were getting hungry, not because we only had 62 rounds!

Ever wonder what a Ferguson Ordnance Rifle looks like after 62 rounds with no maintenance between the shots?

After 62 shots with no cleaning, with no failure to fire due to fouling, and one flint change after the fourth shot. (Lock view)

Top view of same.

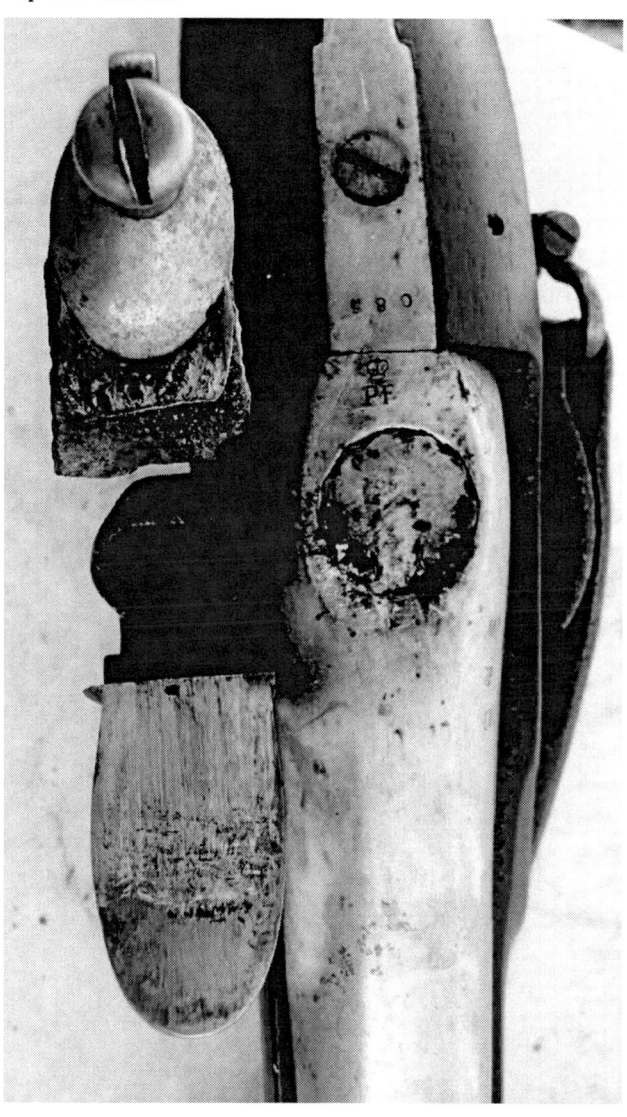

I did not start the day with a new flint; I had one flint change. The black crud around the top of the breech is a mixture of black powder fouling and Fergie-Lube being forced up the breech by the 62 shots.
You do not get this effect when firing 25 or so rounds.

One of the myths about the Ferguson Rifle is that the black powder fouling will cause the rifle to "lock up" after only a few rounds. I believe we can clearly state that this myth is BUSTED!

To create a meaningful comparison, we took three similar rifles to the range: an American long rifle, a Jäger/ Jaeger rifle and a Light Infantry carbine. Using period patch lubricants as appropriate to the arms, we performed torture tests to try to demonstrate *how many shots we could get off without the arm being too difficult to load due to fouling.* You will see references to round bottom and square bottom rifling. Basically these are different shapes of the cutter making the rifling round bottom. Rifling is cut with a tombstone-shaped cutter, which leaves round bottoms in the grooves of the rifling, the theory being that this round bottom is better at moving the fouling. This is more common on original rifles. Square bottom rifling is cut with rectangular cutters and as a result is square in profile. Modern barrels tend to be made this way, as the modern cutter's steel or carbide can hold the sharp corners better than the older high-carbon steel cutters.

Our Results:

Underlined American Long Rifle   10-12 rounds

 Fewer rounds if the barrel was shot and then left to cool, with square bottom rifling.

Jäger Rifle   14-16 rounds

Fewer rounds if the barrel was shot then left to cool, with round bottom rifling.

Light Infantry Carbine   16-18 rounds

Fewer rounds if the barrel was shot then left to cool, smooth bore barrel.

Brown Bess Musket   18-22 rounds

Fewer rounds if the barrel was shot then left to cool, smooth bore barrel.

Ferguson Ordnance Rifle   62 rounds

The fouling was not bad enough to prevent the weapon from shooting further. After using all of the ball we brought with us and spending seven hours on the range we decided to call it a day. Shooting either hot or after being left to cool did not seem to affect the number of rounds with the Ferguson Ordnance Rifle.

Where May I Buy a Ferguson Rifle?

Sadly, Narragansett Arms has long since closed up shop, after manufacturing a limited run of Ferguson Ordnance Rifles. However, you find them now and again on used gun Internet forums and may occasionally find one on a trade blanket at black powder shoots.

Your other option is to craft a Ferguson yourself. Bryan built his Ferguson from parts available from The Rifle Shoppe, Inc. (located in Jones, Oklahoma) since he prefers guns that he builds himself to prefabricated guns. He feels the bond, both physical and emotional, is stronger if you build the gun yourself. Narragansett also used The Rifle Shoppe parts, so if you purchase a parts set from them you are essentially building the same piece. Their Ferguson parts were patterned from the original Ferguson Ordnance Rifle in the collection of the Milwaukee Public Museum. The Ferguson stock we use to demonstrate how weak the wood is was donated to us for our lectures about Patrick Ferguson and his Ordnance Rifle by the fine folks of The Rifle Shoppe. They market a part set for a Ferguson for about $2,000 if you choose to build one yourself (based on 2011 pricing) The Rifle Shoppe, Inc.'s website is http://www.therifleshoppe.com. We do love the quality of their sets and have built a number of pieces using them.

What is the load you use in your Ferguson?

Ball: .615 ball dipped once in melted beeswax or Fergi-lube.

Suggestions for dipping the balls into the lube:

- Ricky uses big tweezers to hold the ball.
- Bryan uses a loop of stiff wire rather like dipping Easter eggs
- Both purchased the molds from Jeff Tanner Moulds in England.

Most of the current information available about the Ferguson rifle does not include a correct ball size. Ricky came to know Jeff Tanner very well over an eight month period by ordering several incorrect molds from him, until we found a proper reference during our research. DeWitt Bailey's *British Military Flintlock Rifles* mentions Ferguson obtaining standard carbine ball for the Ferguson.[72] Now, this is NOT the .648 or .645 caliber ball, nor any other variation of .65 caliber reported by many sources, but is instead the .615 ball, the same standard used by all other British Military rifles and carbines in the 1770-1785 periods.

January, 1777

Capt. Ferguson having requested that the Barrels, Slings, and Bayonets made by him desired may be numbered & scabbards made for the Bayonets also Slings and Bayonet Belts may be of Tann'd Leather and 2 Cags [kegs] of Powder for the Rifles & Carbine Ball]in Proportion sent to Fire at Marks at Chatcham.[73]

A couple of years ago some other Ferguson aficionados gave a Ferguson lecture at the Kings Mountain National Park. They passed around a recovered ball fired from their Ferguson Officers Rifle. They had used the .648 ball as per some modern sources—this ball looked like it swaged through the entire barrel. It had little Sputnik-looking wings where the ball came out of the grooves. We are in no way faulting the gentlemen; they applied what the research at the time dictated. Sadly, it was incorrect, but that is why we keep digging and testing.

The .615 ball does not come close to hitting the bottom of the grooves. The balls retrieved from our tests are perfectly round and the impression of the lands lightly engraved into the lead. This explains why we can shoot this gun until running out of balls without having it foul up. The fouling gathers in the bottom of the grooves. This is exactly why gun makers originally experimented with rifling in 1498, as a physical place for the fouling to go. When you burn black powder, about 80% stays behind as crud. Stabilizing the bullet was a happy and unexpected side effect of the rifling.

Originally the first rifling was straight, not rotating down the bore. Some brush guns still use this straight rifling, colloquially known as a *pumpkin bore*. Initially, the rotation was a technique used by the barrel makers to break fewer cutting tools while making the rifling in the barrel, since the rotating slot cutter was more self-cleaning than the straight slot cutters, which often jammed up or broke. That the spiral rifling also improved accuracy was a happy accident. "Ain't luck grand?"

During the first six months with the rifle, Ricky shot a .648 ball. Even out of a cold barrel, it did not shoot well. The Ferguson rifle did not gain any real accuracy until Ricky tried the .615 ball. He shot much better groups at 100 yards with the .615 ball than he ever did at 50 yards with the larger diameter .648 ball. He also tried .641 and .610 size balls. Although the .610 would not drop through the barrel, since it is smaller than the .615 ball, it shot with about the same accuracy as the .648. Theoretically, a .620 may also work well, but we are very happy with the precision of the .615 British Carbine round and have not tested anything higher.

Muzzle of Ferguson showing rifling.

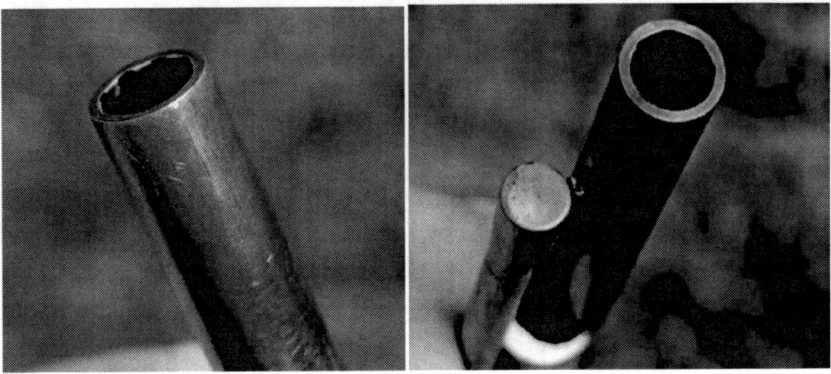

Using the .648 caliber ball, Ricky has fired up to 48 at a time, and they never shot well during any part of the run. The accuracy was just a little better than smoothbore accuracy and a hair better than running ball (spitting loose unpatched balls down the barrel "on the run," a technique used by Native Americans and frontiersmen to maintain a higher volume of fire during a skirmish). Shooting the .648, Ricky never was happy with the accuracy, and was ready to condemn the entire program. The groups did not tighten up until he began shooting the .615 ball.

Every 10th round captured by firing ball into a bundle of wet newspaper

Note how consistent the markings on the ball are, each ball just barely kissed by the rifling. There are no changes due to fouling as would likely be seen on most black powder arms.

Close-up image of balls one and ten

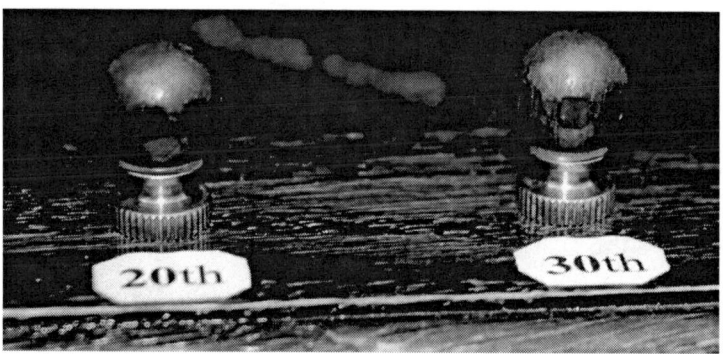

Close-up of balls twenty and thirty

Notice that there is no change in the physical appearance of the balls. This test was conducted with 30 rounds, with no cleaning between shots, using a dipped Fergi-lube breech and lubed ball.

Powder: 65-grain European match grade powder brand rifle (3F) powder (that is what the chamber holds). We use this because we find it offers better performance and less fouling then the traditional black powder. We use traditional United States-produced black powder in most of our other muzzleloaders.

Flints: 1 ⅛ inch long by 1 inch wide (or size 8 at Track of the Wolf, Inc. in Elk River, Minnesota). Knapped flint is our preferred style, or good black English flint when we can find it. Of late, however, we have gotten better performance out of the French Blond flints.

FergiLube: We use our own FergiLube mixture. Here in the Carolinas we find a 70% beeswax and 30% vegetable shortening (2:1) mix works year round. We used to use tallow or salt free lard, but frankly, vegetable shortening was easier to obtain, cheaper, and easier to clean up after shooting. If you are in colder or dryer climates, you may need to move closer to a 50/50 mix. We shoot .615 ball dipped in beeswax (dip once and set aside to dry for a smooth skin, do not let them touch or they grow nibs that get in the way). We also cover the breech plug in the Fergi-Lube as part of both the storage and shooting regimen. We melt the lube and dip the breech into it for optimal performance. But Bryan feels that when cleaning with boiling water the breech is hot enough to melt the FergieLube onto the threads as part of the cleaning process, this performs well enough to prevent fast fouling build up when shooting but not dipping will need reapplication about 25-30 rounds in to your shooting session. So both approaches work, but dipping in molten FergieLube gives the best performance.

With this mix, our current record is 62 rounds. We did not stop due to stiffness or fouling; however, we were hungry and called it quits for the day to go eat! Thus far, running out of ball has consistently been the limiting factor for each of the records; again, running out of ammo to shoot, NOT fouling. We are looking at casting over 100 ball and seeing how long we can continue to shoot (we will be sure to bring snacks that day).

At the 2007 American Long Rifle Association gathering at Fort De Chartres in Illinois there was a "last man standing" match. Three gongs were hung, spread out on a wide frame—a twelve-inch gong, an eight-inch gong, and a four-inch gong (a free-swinging metal target that moves when hit, and makes a loudish gong sound, a nice positive immediate visual and audio feedback mechanism when shooting). The competitors all started their shooting at fifty yards by aiming at the biggest gong, followed by the other gongs. One missed shot meant immediate ejection from the match. They then backed up twenty yards and started over on all three gongs. At the end of this distance there were only two men standing, and Ricky was one of them. They then backed up to the fort road as far as they could go, an approximate distance of more than 80 yards. The final shots came down to the four-inch gong at eighty yards. Even after a long day of shooting, Ricky was able to hit the smaller four-inch targets at eighty yards, winning the competition with the Ferguson rifle!

How does Humidity affect the Ferguson

Humidity in the "winter" here in the Western Carolinas was between 15 and 30 percent on most of the days that we were shooting. A couple of days were 100% and about 40° Fahrenheit when we experienced some winter rainstorms. We did not notice any major difference in performance across the weather spectrum while using the 2:1 Fergi-Lube mix. The thinner mixes we tested melted and seeped out when firing during warmer weather, well above 80° Fahrenheit and 100% humidity. Much thicker mixes became too stiff in below freezing temperatures.

Shooting tips

Safety

You are the guardian of your safety and the safety of those around you. Be Smart, and Be Safe! Please follow all safety guidelines if you are not familiar with shooting black powder arms. We suggest that you take a class; the NRA and NMLRA offer excellent training and safety classes. General safety guidelines can also be found in Appendix A at the back of this book.

Hearing and Eye protection

We are all big boys and girls here, and we are sure everyone knows that ANYTIME you handle a firelock, any firearm, or other tool, hearing and eye protection is essential, but we will remind you anyway. Be Smart, Be Careful! Just because you have two eyes and two ears doesn't mean one is a "spare."

Headgear

Due the escaping gasses from the top of the breech plug, the right type of hat must be worn at all times. The hot gas is expelled in a clockwise swirl that will make you think your forehead is on fire if you are wearing the wrong headgear! The tricorn hat remains Ricky's favorite Fergie hat. The point totally deflects the heat from your forehead. Tying a neckerchief Longhunter-style (on your head like a do-rag or a pirate) also works very well. At times you may end up shooting the Ferguson Rifle at a non-historical event, so here is a selection of other hats with which Bryan and Ricky have had luck:

- A baseball type cap with a bill no longer than 3 inches can be used successfully when firing the Ferguson Ordnance Rifle, as long as the front of the hat is pulled down close to your eyebrows. (Yes Ricky no longer has to turn the hat backwards!).

- Bryan has used his British Light Infantry hat with a 3 ½ inch brim with good success.

The headgear choices have changed since our early results. One thing that has not changed—do not shoot the Ferguson Rifle with a wider brimmed hat (5 inches); this one still hurts!

Ricky likes railroad caps and ear plugs for his "modern ethnic" range attire.

Bryan prefers boonie hats and noise-canceling headphones to protect his ears.

The Sights on the Ferguson Military Rifle

In Ezekiel Baker's book *Baker's Remarks on the Rifle*, published in the early 19th century, the author stated that *"All of the King's Rifles are sighted in at 200 yards."*[74] (This would be a fixed sight, not a flip up sight). This was also the rule of thumb for the 1776 Tower Rifle and at least some of the issued Jaeger Rifles. All of these rifles were sighted in for 18th century European open field combat; 200 yards for the fixed sight and 300 and up for the flip up leaf sights. We have no doubt that the original Ferguson Rifles had their fixed sight set at 200 yards. We are not certain if our modern reproduction Ferguson Rifles have a short powder chamber or if we have not found the right analog to "Double Strength Super Fine" 18th century powder. Because of this, the fixed sight on Ricky's rifle hits dead on at about 160 yards and about 4 inches low at 200 yards. Based on the historical records, original Fergusons would hit dead on at 200 yards.

We have been Ferguson Rifle junkies for many years before either of us owned one. We read accounts from the *Edinburgh Newspaper* of 1775 that reported Capt. Ferguson going into the field with a few of his men to shoot his experimental rifle at 300 yards. Now, despite the fact that Ricky has hit a big gong at 300 yards with a patched round ball out of a stoked up .54 caliber long rifle now and again, he considered this report to be pure propaganda. Surely, this was merely something made up to inject Rebel riflemen with fear about the new British rifle.

After Ricky got his hands on a Ferguson Rifle, he learned a very important lesson—one really should never make snap judgments on something one has never tried! Four times in the last couple of years, Ricky has taken folks to various ranges with longer-range rifle targets and shot his Ferguson Rifle accurately at 300 yards. With the "short" chamber, his Ferguson Rifle shoots a little low at 300 yards. However, you would not want to be a man-sized target at 300 yards and have a Ferguson rifleman aimed at you. Even if the gun shoots a little low at 300 yards with 65 grains of powder and a greased ball, can there be any doubt of where the original rifles would hit using the flip up sight and either a "full depth" powder chamber or the correct powder!

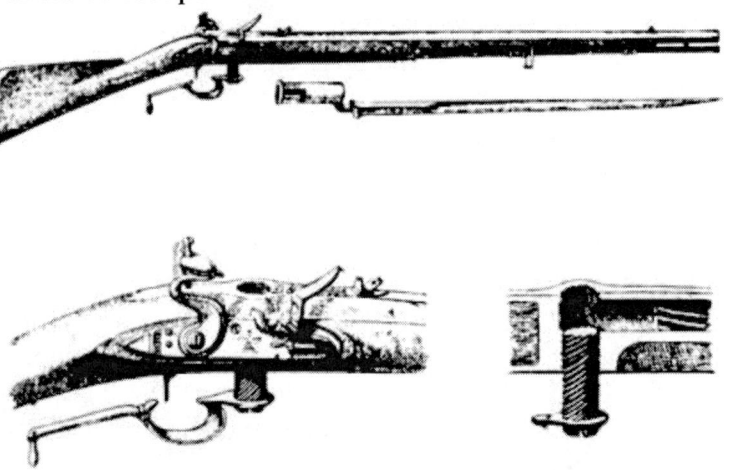

19th century images of the Ferguson Rifle from Adam Fergusons 1817 article for the Encyclopedia

Ferguson's Rifles and the British Army

We have shown the positive and negative aspects of Patrick Ferguson's Breech Loading Ordnance Rifle. We are now left with one question: why didn't the British support Patrick Ferguson's rifle program? The excuse "because the British did not use rifles" is not terribly convincing. Here is why:

- King Henry VIII did have access to rifles. He personally owned a German wheel lock rifle that fired compound loads. Compound loads fire multiple shots stacked one on top of the other. This was a not terribly effective, if common, attempt at multiple shots in the muzzle-loading era.

- Thirty rifled Carbines were requested to be sent along on Lord Cathcart's expedition to the Caribbean in 1740, but as noted in the record, *"Wall guns* [were] *sent in lieu of."* [75]

- In 1746, General Arthur St. Clair had 60 rifles with him, possibly of German origin, when relieving Louisburg. The records show an additional 50 rifled carbines sent along with the follow-on artillery train. In addition, the French records of Quebec show 5 rifled Carbines in 1743, possibly French 1733 pattern rifled dragoon carbines. [76]

- The British had approximately 1200 model 1776/1777 Tower Rifles in the American colonies during the Revolution. Eight hundred of them were delivered before the first Ferguson was produced. The British Crown forces had rifled arms as part of the establishment 1757 and 1762 pattern rifles as well. The Hessian Jaeger riflemen in the service of the British Crown had over 1,000 of their own rifles and were issued Pistor pattern Jaeger rifles.

- When the British won a battle or skirmish and captured American rifles, they were often given to Loyalist rifle companies.

Therefore, it can be said with some certainty that the British did use rifles.

The five things the British did not like about the American long rifle:

1. It did not mount a bayonet. In the 18th century, the bayonet ruled the battlefield. Victory was not measured by casualties but by who was able to retain the field of battle. Rifles could project power, but they could not hold against bayonets or mounted troops.

2. It was very slow to load. The tighter patched loads for a rifle significantly slowed loading. Where a well-drilled soldier could fire 3-5 times a minute with a musket, a rifle did well to get off one or two patched ball in that same time. The idea that riflemen could just snipe away and kill all the Regulars does not hold water. A line of infantry advancing covers an area the size of a football field about every minute and ten seconds. If a rifleman has 300 yards to make his shots, he can only fire 6 rounds maximum before the point of the bayonet arrives. What is more, they have taken three volleys of musket fire in that time as well. Unless protected by regular line infantry, rifles simply cannot hold a field.

3. It was expensive in terms of both cost and labor. While rifles were more widespread in Pennsylvania and down south through the Carolinas, they were not so common in New England. Even in the rifle-friendly Southern colonies, smoothbore fowlers are more commonplace, in part because a smooth bore barrel is cheaper to produce than a rifled barrel. Labor-wise, an 18th century rifling

machine requires walking approximately sixty miles to hand rifle one barrel, in a twelve to sixteen-foot round trip. One or two laps, shim the cutter, repeat for around 19,800 laps.

4. It has a very fragile stock. The stock is quite thin on a long rifle and really does not handle the abuses of military life very well.

5. It did not shoot what they considered a man-stopping, military caliber ball. They considered .60 caliber or higher military bore, 50 caliber to be a light hunting arm for midsize game, and smaller bore to be for squirrel guns.

Some other thoughts on why the Ferguson was not adopted by the British:

1. Cost –The Ferguson rifle cost £4 to manufacture versus £1.1.0 for a Brown Bess. In comparison the expense for black powder was significantly more for the Ferguson. The Ferguson shot "Glazed" or "Super Fine Double Strength" powder, which cost £7.10.0 per barrel, whereas the Brown Bess shot common musket powder at £1.5.0 per barrel.

They had bean counters in 1776, just as they do today. The gun was four times more expensive to build, it has two times higher maximum rate of fire of the musket, and the cost of "consumables" per shot was seven times higher. The British army in the modern era did not move from bolt action rifles to semi-automatic rifles until 1951, when they adopted the FN-FAL (L1A1) in semi-auto (1 trigger pull 1 bullet fired) ONLY, not selective fire (1 trigger pull fires multiple rounds). The British Army would not issue a selective-fire or full-auto weapon to their regular army troops until the 1980's with the Enfield L85A1. This was due in part to concerns on the part of the exchequer and general staff that full-auto weapons might result in profligate waste of ammunition. This was the same argument the Union brass used during the Civil War so as not to move to metallic cartridge repeating arms for all the infantry; they issued muzzleloaders and paper cartridges for most troops.

Add to this the fact that in the 1770s the British treasury was already depleted from the French and Indian or Seven Years' War, when defending the colonies from French incursion. This dug deep into the Crown's coffers, and Parliament was not of a mind to spend money from their war chest on the military.

2. The Brown Bess Short and Long land pattern muskets were still relatively "new" in their projected 50-year service life, and the costs to replace 50,000 would have been brutal on the already stretched Crown treasury. Also, with pre-industrial "cottage" manufacturing British gun makers would max out production at approximately 1,000 units per year. Scholars estimate it took gun makers an extra 1.5 days per gun to build a Ferguson versus a Brown Bess. In large part this is why breechloaders did not catch on until the Industrial Revolution took place in the early 19th century. Manufacturing techniques had not yet caught up to the technology.[77]

3. The Ferguson rifle has a rather weak stock where the massive breech passes through the wood. Every one of the original Ferguson rifles in museums has repairs in this area. Even Ferguson Ordnance Rifle #2, which is the one Pattie demonstrated in front of the king (and which is now stored in the Tower of London), has a repair in this area. Eighteenth

century soldiers were very rough on their firelocks. Per the *British Manual of Arms* of 1764 the British soldiers were trained to slam the butts of their muskets on the ground to make the ground shake and their ramrods rattle. The Ferguson Rifle was too delicate for this sort of abuse!

Ricky has been shooting his Ferguson for several years now, and treats it like a squirrel gun! Perhaps if Ferguson had incorporated Clarkson's all metal breech section and 2-part stock into his other improvements, the Ferguson Ordnance Rifle might have caught on with the Crown Forces.[78]

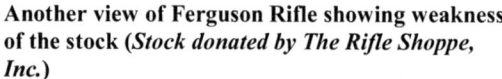

Another view of Ferguson Rifle showing weakness of the stock (*Stock donated by The Rifle Shoppe, Inc.*)

4. Tallow. Each rifle had to have tallow on the threads and ball to operate smoothly. The vision of Ferguson running through the British camp prior to Brandywine scrounging all the tallow he could find still troubles us. Keep in mind though, this would have been common among all rifles in the Crown forces, though the Ferguson probably needed a larger quantity to remain operational.

5. The breech opens up after one full turn. If you slip up and make two turns the breech falls out on the ground. You now have a pike, no longer a shooting weapon. The breeches were hand fitted to the rifle; they were not interchangeable. The "one turn to load and two to remove" was a marked improvement over some other designs (Ferguson was not the first to use "starting threads"). However, this would still be an issue without adequate training to develop proper muscle memory.

6. The Ferguson rifle used a high grade, high cost German powder (Super Fine Double Strength/Glazed Powder—like the Jäger and Tower rifles in Crown service). This was very costly and had to be exported to the British Isles from the Germanic states.

7. The Ferguson Rifle used standard carbine flints so as to better take advantage of the existing Crown supply system.

Other attempts at breechloaders

Why breechloaders? Basically, loading a *muzzle-loading* arm is something of a juggling match, and then pouring powder in at one end. Then one must set the patch and ball, ram them down, and then returning to the stock, reverse the rammer twice in the process, priming the other end and then bring the whole bit back to the shoulder to fire. This as opposed to a *breech loader*, where all the action is well at the breech, with a lot less juggling about. This allows you to shoot much faster and, well, we all know being able to shoot faster is something of an obsession with firearms enthusiasts throughout time.

Various 18th century gunsmiths were also working on their own designs for breechloaders, some in the British Isles and other on the Continent. These included Willits, Chaumette, Bidet, Hirst, Wassup, among others.

Not Just Flintlocks

Breech-loading cannons such as the Hackebucshe are described in Leonardo da Vinci's *Codex Atlantica.*[79] Moreover, such arms were common in the time of Henry VIII, such as on his flagship the *Mary Rose*, which had breech-loading cannons mounted on its decks. As the Hackebucshe cannons fell out of favor, their chargers, or cartridges, maintained an afterlife as "thunder mugs" a signaling device and festival noisemaker.

Bryan's Thundermug

Flintlocks

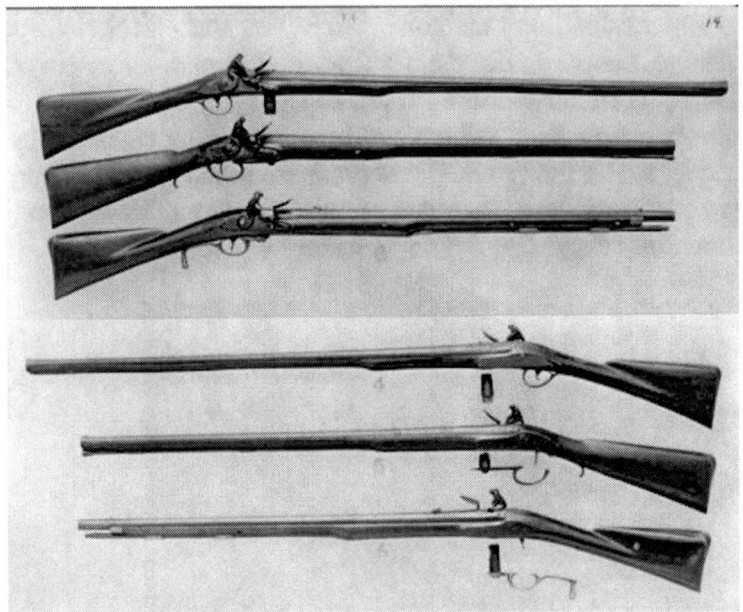

Numbers 1 & 4 are a Hirst Breechloader N7151 and a Hadley rifle; 2 & 5 are Chaumette Breechloader N6196 and a Foster rifle; and numbers 3 & 6 are a Ferguson Breechloader. (*Images courtesy Milwaukee Public Museum*)

Bidet Breech- loading Flintlock

Bidet used the simple screw breech in his arm, which required four rotations to open the breech for loading. At 4 ¼ to 4 ½ rotations (it varies some based on specific examples) the breech plug comes out completely; thus it is not terribly forgiving to any nervousness or fumbling during battle, or getting off a faster second shot while hunting.

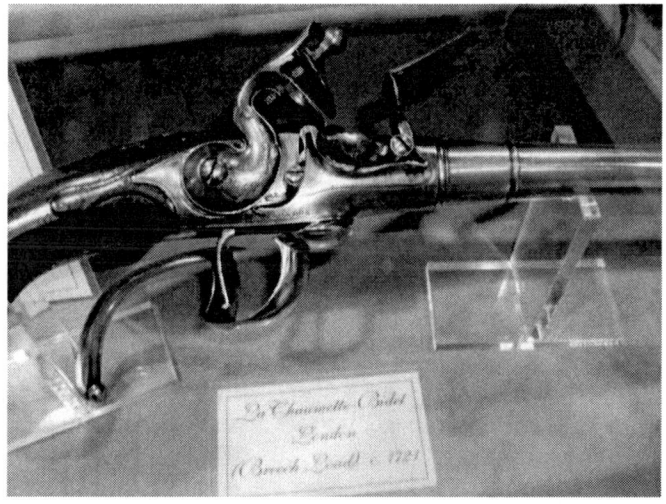

Bidet Pistol (*From the collection of John B. Chalapis*)

Bidet Pistol (*From the collection of John B. Chalapis*)

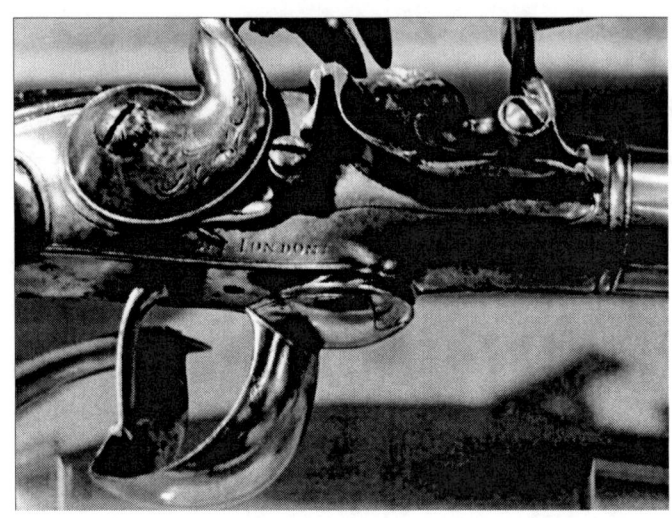

Close up image of **Bidet Pistol** (*From the collection of John B. Chalapis*)

Chaumette Breechloader

Chaumette's system (see below) improved upon Bidet's, with an extended breech column requiring five full rotations to remove the breech, although this still was an awkward arrangement. The multiple rotations required counting, to fully open the breech without removing the breech plug entirely. Chaumette was a French Huguenot who fled to England during the persecution of Protestants, also known as the French Counter Reformation, and continued building arms after his arrival there.

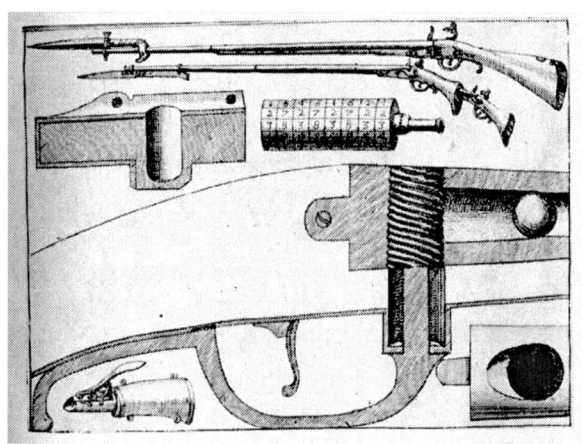

Excerpt from a leaflet explaining Chaumette's Designs as covered by his English patent of 1721 (*Public domain image*) [80]

Isaac de La Chaumette of Paris presented his breech-loading system to the Académie des Sciences in Paris in the year 1704, but afterwards immigrated to London, where he patented his invention in 1721. Parisian examples were produced by Brion and Bourgeois. Captain Patrick Ferguson later improved the Chaumette system in 1776.

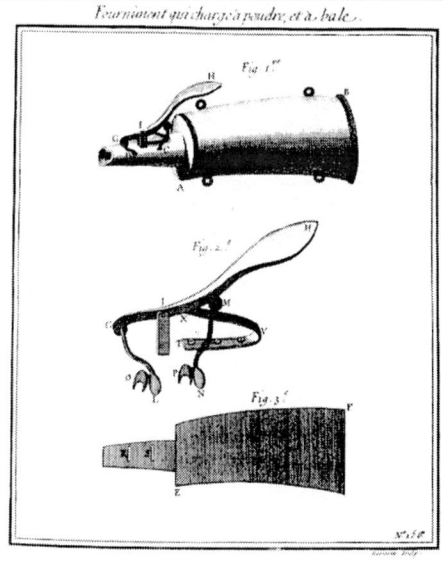

Chaumette's double-acting flask for powder and ball patented in 1715 in London (*Public domain image*) [81]

This design was not intended to load both powder and ball simultaneously but rather to measure out how either was deployed in two different flasks.

Willets Breech "Baker" Hunting Rifle

This is a piece Bryan and Ricky were asked to examine while it was on display at a regional museum. It is a pumpkin bore (straight rifling, no twist), breech- loading rifle made by Englishman Ezekiel Baker of Baker Rifle fame. This is NOT a Ferguson pattern rifle, even though it postdates the Ferguson, and Baker was aware of it. It uses a Willets-pattern screw breech, which is basically a Bidet Breech with anti-fouling notches.

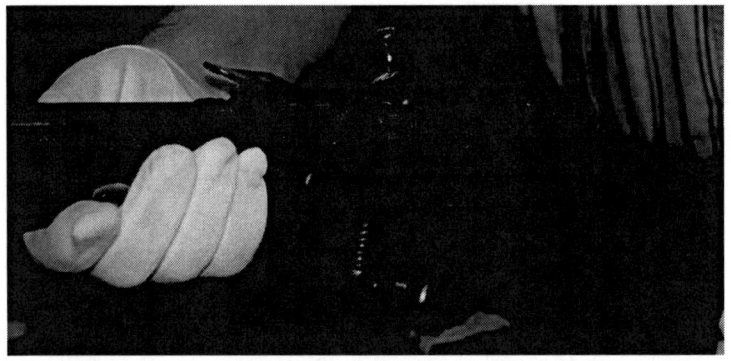

Willets Breech "Baker" Rifle

This design uses simple threads, not a starting thread arrangement, thus requiring multiple turns of the trigger guard to open the action.

Willets Breech "Baker" Rifle

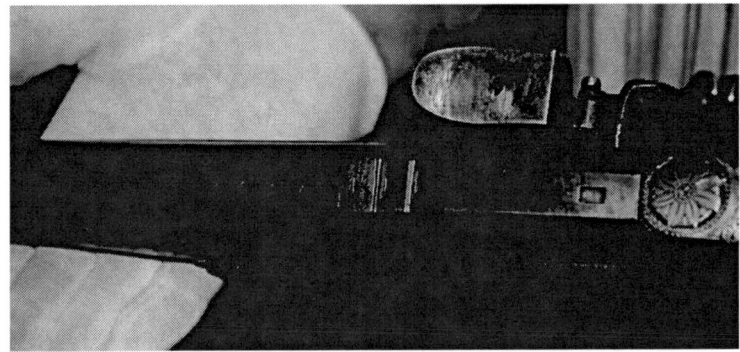

Willets Breech "Baker" Rifle

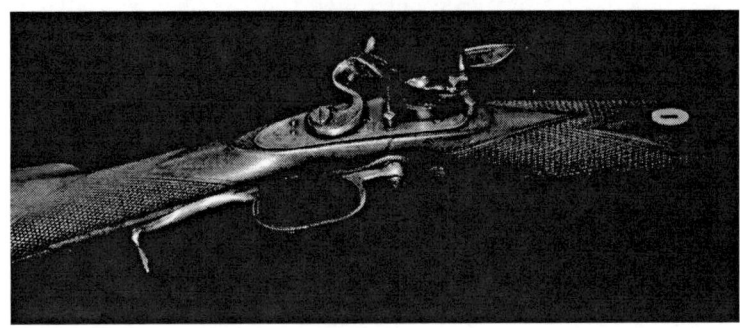

Willets Breech "Baker" Rifle

Willets Breech "Baker" Rifle

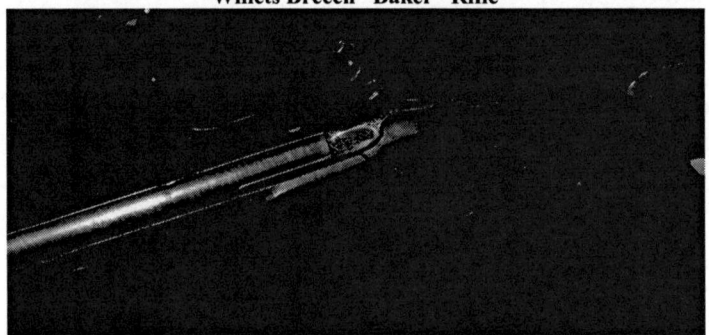

Willets Breech "Baker" Rifle

"Ezekiel Baker London" stamped on top barrel flat on Willets Breech "Baker" Rifle

A Brief History of the Rifle

History of the Rifle

Important Dates in Firearms History

- The invention of gunpowder took place on various dates, in various locations, relatively simultaneously. It may have been independently discovered in different locales, but most likely came to Europe with Muslim traders importing silk and technology from China. Some say China invented it in the 10th century; others credit Roger Bacon in the 11th century, while some credit Bertold Swartz, a German Monk, in the 12th century (who incidentally is credited with the first bronze cannon). Since, the first recorded uses of gunpowder in Europe predate Swartz's "discovery" by about 100 years, and there being no real evidence that he ever really existed, merely being a creature of legend, this can be discounted.
- The first record of the actual use of gunpowder in Europe is a statement by Bishop Albertus Magnus in 1280 that it was used during the Siege of Seville in 1247.
- Hand cannon and ribaldiquinn (a medieval volley gun) appeared in the field of battle during the reign of Edward III in 1364, and were significant in his victory at Crecy against the French.
- We hear of armor being penetrated by bullets and the hand gun showing signs of becoming a weapon capable of rudimentary precision by 1425.
- Henry VII organized the corps of Yeomen of the Guard, half of whom were to carry bows and arrows while the other half were equipped with harquebuses. This represents the first introduction of firearms as an official weapon of the Royal Guard in 1485.
- Rifling was invented in 1498.
- Rifled military arms have been made since 1540.
- The hair trigger was a German invention of about 1540.

- The standard flintlock gun came in about 1630.
- The screw or cannon barrel pistol probably came into use prior to 1640.
- The earliest known English breech-loading rifle was made by Willmore, who was apprenticed to Foad in 1689.
- Patrick Ferguson patented his "Improvements in breech loading firearms" in 1776.

Rifles Used in the British Army in the 18th Century

- 1757 Pattern   Cost 3£   Muzzleloader; no known example
- 1762 Pattern Breechloader [82]   Cost 7£   Hirst Pattern
- 1776 Pattern Muzzleloader [83]   Cost £ 6.10.0   Hanoverian made
- 1776/7 Pattern made Muzzleloader [84]   Cost £ 3.2.0   Grice (Birmingham)
- Ferguson Ordnance D. Egg   Cost £ 31.10   Master Pattern Pieces
- Ferguson Ordnance   Cost £4   (Gun makers Grice & Son wanted an additional £4 per gun as well as late as 1777, but did not receive it).
- Super Fine Double Strength Powder
  Cost £ 7.10.0 per barrel
- Musket Powder   Cost £ 1.5.0 per barrel
- There is clear evidence of at least 1,000 British Rifles existing in the Americas at the start of the Revolution (not counting the rifles brought in with Hessian forces). The maximum we can document is about 100 Ferguson Ordnance Rifles deployed with the Crown forces in the American Colonies.[85]

How was bore size expressed in the period?

The short answer is in the number of balls to a pound of lead, which is the equivalent of "gauge" as is used on most modern shotguns, the exception being the .410, which is .41 caliber—go figure. .75 cal = 11 balls/lb., and .69 cal = 15 balls/lb., though these are usually rounded off to their modern shotgun equivalents of 12 & 16 gauge, respectively. However, the period method would be to refer to it as an 11 bore rather than a 12 gauge. Some of the more common ones (roughly rounded off) are:

Gauge Bore Balls per Pound	Caliber	Weight grains
8	0.835	875
10	0.776	700
12	0.73	583
13	0.71	538
14	0.693	500
16	0.663	438
20	0.615	350
24	0.579	292
28	0.55	292

While "caliber" was a period term in the 18th century, it was used by the artillery as a measure of the relative length of a gun barrel, and was defined as the length divided by the diameter of the bore. Thus, a 50-caliber gun on a warship had a barrel 50 times longer than its bore. Confining the shell within the barrel as it fires for a longer time increases the velocity, so guns with a higher caliber usually have a longer range.

We are not sure precisely when the bore size was first expressed in hundredths of an inch, which is how it is expressed today. In England the use of bore versus caliber seems to have been the norm through at least the 1850s. There was probably some overlap of use as one form of expression fell out of favor and the other became more main stream.

To make the term "bore" even more challenging; its interpretation can vary depending on the culture and country in question. As a result you have to take care when comparing English arms to French, Dutch, etc., since the "pound" used to determine bore is not always the same.

- Modern 21st century "Pound"/18th century English/American "Pound" 1.0   Pound = 453.59 Grams
- French 18th Century "Pound" 1.0 Pound = 489 Grams
- Dutch 18th Century "Pound" 1.0 Pound = 494.09 Grams
- German (Prussia) 18th Century "Pound" 1.0 Pound =   467.4 Grams
- Danish 18th Century "Pound" 1.0 Pound = 500 Grams
- Swedish 18th Century "Pound" 1.0 Pound = 425.08 Grams

These differences in units of measure become especially important when trying to compare firelocks, as bore is a function of how many ball to the local "pound." The table above is in "modern" pound equivalents. This makes interpreting period documents just that much more fun!

They didn't have set triggers back then?

Actually, the set trigger has been in use since at least 1540. You can find set triggers used on wheel lock arms up to the modern cartridge arms.

Importance of powder and its power

Manufacturing, such as it was in the 18th century, was not quite up to modern standards. Every batch of powder a shooter purchased or received had to be tested for quality and for power to be certain that it would shoot the way the shooter expected it to. The tool used in making these tests was called an eprouvette, or powder tester. It was a plate held by either a mass or a spring of some kind that allowed a known volume of powder to measure for energy against a standard scale. It was not uncommon for merchants and shippers to adulterate the powder to increase their profit margins, or the makers to substitute the proper willow charcoal ingredient with cheaper grades of oak or pine charcoal, or even coal dust. Mixing in these contaminants to the powder slows the burn to the point that it is no longer gunpowder, but rather a rocket propellant (more whoosh than boom, and utterly useless for shooting purposes).

Gun powder manufactories in the Americas at the time of the American Revolution were very primitive even by 18th century powder standards and much of the powder was not even caked or corned during manufacture. This meant that the ingredients—sulfur, potassium nitrate and charcoal—were mixed dry, and could possibly settle out into their component layers inside the barrels. At that point the materials would have to be recombined, either by the quartermaster or the gun crews, before they could be fired. In contrast, the 18th century British army was shooting "modern" corned powder, where the manufacturer wet-caked the powder to create a single amalgamated dough-like structure and then reground the new amalgam to make the various grades of powder. In addition, the British rifles had the new super-high-tech Germanic "Super Fine Double Strength" or "Double Glazed" powder, a grade of powder that the English and the French would not learn how to manufacture until the early 19th century. The low to middling quality of the powder available in the colonies was an important factor in the style and evolution of the American longrifle.

The American Long rifle and Jaeger/Military Rifle. Which is better?

In our discussions, presentations and research on black powder arms in general, and rifles in particular, we are often asked which was the best rifle of the period: the Jaeger Rifle, the American Long rifle, or some other? This is a more complicated question to answer than one might suspect.

Bryan Brown's twist lock Jaeger Rifle

James Van Ness's fine Chiseled Jaeger Rifle

Ricky Roberts's Pistor Jaeger

Let us begin with the origins of these arms. The Jaeger Rifle was developed by hunters who were traveling a few days at most in the woods, hunting VERY large game such as Red Deer (elk), Russian Boar, and huge Grey Wolves (they were uncommon in the 18th century but not completely unheard of), often at great distances. Rifles were born in southern central Europe, in the Trans-Alpine regions; shots of 200-400 yards in the mountains are not uncommon. Lead mines are common throughout this part of the world. So with a big bore rifle with energy to go through game and take them down faster the cost of the lead isn't a factor as it would be for American

Long rifles. Natural lead deposits are relatively common in Europe, but there were no commercial lead mines in the Americas until the 19th century. A few small ones here and there, and one in VA that would remain a State secret until after the US Civil War. This meant that the vast majority of lead shot in the American Colonies had to be imported from Europe, especially for large dangerous game like Russian Boar and Grey Wolves. Furthermore, these rifles evolved from smoothbore firearms and Newton's Second Law rules smoothbores: "A mass in motion stays in motion unless acted upon by an external force." In round ball projectiles, with equal energy (powder), bigger balls shoot farther, straighter and hit harder than smaller ball. And you thought size didn't matter!

Ball size comparisons from musket down to small rifle

This is why *military* muskets are a larger caliber (also referred to as bore size) than *militia* muskets, which are larger caliber than trade guns for colonists, which are, in turn, larger caliber than trade guns for local natives. The larger caliber gives each level an advantage in range and knockdown power over the gun in the level beneath it.

Ricky Roberts's Long Rifle. This rifle was made by Mike Miller of Paducah, Kentucky

165

The American longrifle sprang from the roots of the Germanic Jaeger Rifles and French Fusil de Chasse (light hunting smoothbores). There is a 1705 receipt for a "rifle-gun" made by a gunsmith in what is now Berks County, Pennsylvania, so we know rifles have been made in the American colonies since at least 1705.

The longrifles evolved into a longer and lighter hunting arm for several reasons. First, the long hunters were just that, they did not go out hunting for a few days and then return to hearth and home. They undertook long hunts, and were perhaps gone for weeks or months at a time. They commonly hunted for pelts or hides to sell to traders who eventually took the raw hides back to the European markets.

Their weapon needed to be a lighter arm which a man could carry every day, all day, for weeks or months, often while transporting very heavy loads. The Hawken style of rifle gained popularity in the 19th century because the rising standard of living meant more folks could afford pack horses to help carry heavy game. The long rifle is a weapon designed for a hunter on foot who carried much of his kit.

We touched earlier on the low quality of powder made here in the Americas during the Revolution, but the longrifles' evolution began before that era. Colonists were generally shooting British-made musket grade powder or trade powder, a rather coarse slower-burning powder, compared to the high tech "rifle" powders of the day. Much of this powder was militia issue powder, which had been reported "lost" or "spoiled." This was a shared lie, as the militia officers did not care about the technical fraud; the more their troops practiced, the better shots they became, whether shooting at marks or shooting for supper. Besides, unlike Crown officers, the cost of running the regiment did not come out of an individual's pocket, but instead the province's coffers. Some of the powder was trade grade—the same powder everyone else shot in their fowlers. This slow-burning powder needed more barrel length to capture the energy of the burning powder and transfer it to the ball. This encouraged the design of the longer barrels we see on long rifles, muskets and fowlers; they require the longer barrel because of the type of powder being fired.

There were very few lead mines in the colonies in the 18th century, so almost every shot fired was ball cast from lead imported from Europe. Hunters were willing to invest time in tracking game to keep the ball embedded in the game. A recovered ball could be recast and shot again (and you thought recycling was a new concept). In addition, ranges in the forests of North America tended to be 75-150 yards; you rarely needed to shoot farther than that for 90% of all your shooting in the colonies. If you kept the ball in the game, you were able to recapture it and re-melt it to use again, since pure lead is a fungible commodity and can be repeatedly melted and reused.

In old beef shoots where competitors bought chances to fire at marks (targets) to take a chance at winning part of a beef cow or other prizes, first place was the meat and offal. Second place was the hide, horns, and hooves, and third place got to dig the lead out of the backstop. There are even instances of first and second place winners trading the third place winner for the lead. People could raise their own cattle, but they could not grow lead. This frugality helped to model the long rifle to use smaller caliber (or bore in period parlance) which allows for the slimmer graceful lines we have come to expect from it.

Military rifles are very specialized tools for hunting only one sort of game, i.e., man. In the 18th century, military rifles tended to be in the Jaeger rifle model, though some like the Ferguson Breechloader shoot carbine ball at .62 caliber. For the purposes of this discussion, we lump them into the Jaeger rifle school of influence, versus the longrifle School.

So which rifle is "better"? Well, frankly, they both are perfect. Perfect for the job they evolved to do, and the role they were designed to serve. It is really very much like trying to say what is better—a hammer or a screwdriver. Different tools with different jobs, both perfect in their own way.

Conclusion

We hope that you have enjoyed reading our exploration of history as much as we enjoying discovering it and sharing it with you. We have tried to make Patrick Ferguson come to life so that you have a better grasp of him as a real person. No doubt you now have a better understanding of the man and his fascinating bit of 18th century technology. It is our hope that you found our discussions of the technologies of the 18th century, especially when comparing rifles and muskets and sharing some of the background of the technologies, of use. If you enjoyed reading this work, and learned a little something, we count ourselves lucky and well pleased with the results.

If we have fanned your interest in history into a little brighter flame please read some of the other works we mention. Also consider attending a living history event in your area, and continue to explore your own areas of interest and discuss them with others. Ricky and Bryan came so much further with their research and experimentation working together and sharing information with each other than either would have achieved while working on their own.

Learning is fun and contagious—share it!

Appendix A: Safety Guidelines

DISCLAIMER: In providing the information in this book to you the authors and publisher make no warranty, express or implied, as to the validity or suitability of the information. Any actions you take are your responsibility, since only you are the guardian of your safety and the safety of those around you.

PLEASE READ AND UNDERSTAND THE FOLLOWING:

- **Treat every gun as if it were loaded. Have your muzzle under control at all times and keep it pointed down range.**
- **Use ONLY black powder in muzzleloaders and other non-metallic cartridge firearms. Modern gunpowder generates much higher pressures and can burst your barrel, injuring you or others who may be nearby.**
- **Make sure your firing mechanism is clean and the firearm is functioning properly *before* loading and that your load is firmly seated on the powder *before* pulling the trigger.**
- **Drop your rammer down the barrel to be sure it is empty (it should "ping") before your first load and after your last load of the day.**
- **Wear ear and eye protection when shooting -- *even if it is not authentic to the period.***
- **Never drink alcoholic beverages while handling firearms, or before handling firearms.**
- **Be VERY CAUTIOUS of a misfire, hang fire or flash in the pan. Your gun is still live and can still discharge even after several minutes. Keep the muzzle pointed down range and wait one full minute before re-priming and trying again. If you still have a misfire, pour water into the pan and down the barrel (keeping hands and face well clear) before attempting to pull the load.**
- **Never smoke when shooting or hunting. Be very cautious with powder horns, measures and related shooting**

accessories when near fire or open flame. Always replace the plug in your horn before firing.

- Be sure of your target and know what is down range *behind* your target. When hunting, know where the other members of your party are and NEVER fire over their heads—even if they drop down and tell you to do so!
- Keep your muzzle up, clear of your hunting partners, and NEVER take the field with your weapon at full-cock. Only go to full-cock when you are on target, or, if hunting, after the game flushes. (Several people have experienced accidental discharge because a twig, blade of grass or sudden jar tripped the trigger. This may seem an inconvenience, but a missed bird or two could save someone's life!)

We have no control over your actions on the shooting range or conditions in the field and we cannot be held responsible for accidents--THINK before you shoot and exercise caution and use common sense at all times.

THE ONLY SAFETY ON ANY FIREARM IS YOU!!!

Be Smart, be safe!

YOU are responsible for the safety of yourself and those around you!

Safety first!

If you are new to shooting live rounds from a muzzle-loading firearm, PLEASE find someone to show you how to properly and SAFELY load and shoot. *We* offer the following information only as a guide. YOU are responsible for your own safety and the safety of those around you when shooting.

Safety classes can be found through the National Rifle Association or National Muzzle Loading Rifle Association at their websites:

http://www.nra.org

http://www.nmlra.org/education.asp

Appendix B: Ferguson and the Brandywine shot

Whilest Knyphausen was forming the Line within a mile of the Rebell camp to wait for G Howes attack, their Rifle men were picking off our men very fast by random Shots from a wood some hundred yards in front as it is easy to do execution upon such large objects (I had only 20 men with me (a few having been disabled by the Enemy the rest from fatigue) who however proved Sufficient for my Lads first dislodged them from the skirts of the wood then drove them from a breastwork within it after which our purpose being answered we lay down at the further skirt of the wood not unnecessarily to provock an attack being so few without Support We had not layn long when a Rebell Officer remarkable by a Huzzar Dress passed towards our Army within 100 yards of my right flank, not perceiving us - he was followed by another dressed in dark green on blue mounted on a very good bay horse with a remarkable large high cocked hat I ordered three good shots to steal near them and fire at them but the idea disgusted me and I recalled them. The Huzzar in returning made a Circuit, but the other passed within 100 yards of us, upon which I advanced from the wood towards him; Upon my calling he stopd, but after looking at me proceeded. I again drew his attention and made signs to him to Stop, levelling my piece at him; but he slowly continued his way. As I was within that distance at which in the quickest firing I have seldom misst a Sheet of paper and Could have lodged half a dozen of balls in or about him before he was out of my reach I had only to determine but it was not pleasant to fire at the back of an inoffending individual who was acquitting himself very coolly of his duty so I let him alone - The day after I had Just been telling this Story to some wounded Officers who lay in the same room with me, when one of our surgeons (who had been dressing the wounded Rebell Officers) came in and told us that they had been informing him that General Washington was all morning with the Light Troops generally in their front and only attended by a french Officer in a huzzar dress he himself mounted and dressed as above described; The oddness of their dress had puzzled me and made me take notice of it. I am not sorry that I did not know all the time who it was.

Dictated journal paper, to unidentified recipient, 31 January 1778, Philadelphia:
[Edinburgh University Library, Laing MSS, La 11, 456; probably associated with letter to John Home or Hume, c. February 1778, in same collection]
Duplicate of Scrymgeour-Wedderburn Papers, NRA(S) 783, 140/2/89, save for minor variants in spelling and punctuation, but signed in own hand. [86]

Appendix C: Memorials and Epitaphs

A poem by Mr. Woodward, from *The Edinburgh Gazette*, 8 May 1781, transcribed by Betty Scrymgeour-Wedderburn:

From the Edin^r Gazette of May 8th – 1781

Epitaph on Major Patrick Ferguson

Here Soldiers sighing o'er a Heros grave tell how he fought & dy'd; and Genius bends Mourning the Patriot worth She could not save whilst Social friendship weeps the best of friends and Bleeding pity viewing what is done in Silent woe, laments her darling Son: For Sure the gentlest warrior here is laid, whose generous Soul no evil e'er repaid: whose noble Breast no Selfish passion Stained for there the chastest love of Glory reigned whose martial ardour tenderest feelings crowned And but too daring, not a fault was found let honour pay the debt his actions claim,Let Candour give to distant times his fame, Let Grateful Britons, to their Hero just, with never

fading laurels Shade his dust: his gallant deeds to future Soldiers tell
teach them like him in Glory to excel: for this he fought for this Alas!
he fell.

wrote by M[r] Woodward[87]

"Biographical Article for the British Encyclopaedia",
handwritten extract:

Ferguson Major Patrick, killed in the action at Kings
Mountain South Carolina 7th Oct[r] 1780. The esteem and love of his
fellow Officers dictated the following Epitaph, which was inserted in
the New York Gazett - 14th July 1781
If an ardent thirst for military fame,
A social and benevolent Heart,
An uncommon Genius,
A mind glowing with Patriotick fire
Replete with usefull knowledge
And capable of persevering under difficulties
when Glory was in view
Claim our admiration
The fate of Major Patrick Ferguson
who possessed these and other virtues
In an eminent degree,
And who fell warring against discord,
Iresistibly Claims our Tears.[88]

Appendix D: Egg Harbor

Copy of Casimir Pulaski's letter to Congress after his defeat at Egg Harbor, New Jersey dated 16 October 1778, with riposte by 'Egg-Shell' (Patrick Ferguson), published in *The Royal Gazette* (James Rivington, New York), No. 220, Saturday 7 November 1778, page 3:

New-York, November 7.

Extract of a letter from General Count Polaski, to the President of the Congress, dated October 16, 1778.

"SIR,

For fear that my first letter concerning my engagement should miscarry or be delayed, and having other particulars to mention, I thought proper to send you this letter.

"You must know that one Juliet an officer, lately deserted from the enemy, went off to them two days ago, with three men whom he debauched and two others whom they forced with them, the enemy excited without doubt by this Juliet, attacked us the 15th instant, at three o'clock in the morning, with 400 men. They seemed at first to attack our pickets and infantry with fury, who lost a few men in retreating; then the enemy advanced to our infantry. The Lieutenant Colonel Baron de Bose, who headed his men and fought vigorously, was killed with several bayonet wounds, as well as the Lieutenant de la Borderie, and a small number of soldiers and others were wounded. This slaughter would not have ceased so soon, if on the first alarm I had not hastened with my cavalry to support the infantry, which then kept a good countenance. The enemy soon fled in great disorder, and left behind them a great quantity of arms, accoutrements, hats, blades, &c.

"We took some prisoners and should have taken many had it not been for a swamp through which our horses could scarce walk: Notwithstanding this we still advanced in hopes to come up with them, but they had taken up the planks of a bridge for fear of being

overtaken, which accordingly saved them; however, my light-infantry and particularly the company of rifle-men, got over the remains of the plank and fired some vollies on their rear. We had the advantage and made them run again, although they were more in number.

"I would not permit my hunters to pursue any further, because I could not assist them, and they returned again to our line, without any loss at that time.

"Our loss is estimated, dead, wounded and absent, about 25 or 30 men, and some horses. That of the enemy appears to be much more considerable. We had cut of the retreat of about 25 men, who retired into the country and the woods, and we cannot find them; the general opinion is, that they are concealed by the tories in the neighbourhood of this encampment."

In Congress, 17th October, 1778.

>   *Ordered to be published,*
>   *HENRY LAURENS, President.*
>   *To the PRESIDENT of the CONGRESS.*

> *SIR,*
> *AS you have thought proper to favour the public with a letter from General Comte Polaski, in explanation of one previously wrote by that gentleman, concerning what he is pleased to call his late engagement; (altho' I have generally understood that term to imply a little fighting) and as the second letter, which alone has been produced, leaves the public almost as much at a loss as that which remains buried in the dark and hollow bosom of the Congress; give me leave to present you with a few remarks, until the Comte shall be pleased to do it the justice he meant for the first, by sending an interpretation of his own to attend upon it.*

> *First then, sir, - Had not the Comte, by the bad choice of his cantonments and neglect of measures necessary for their security, invited an enemy to insult him with a certainty of impunity, persons coming from him could scarce have prevailed upon a small detachment of foot, without either artillery or support, to have committed itself in a country so near the imperial seat of the mighty Congress, among a body of foot, horse and field artillery, known to*

be many times its number, exclusive of the militia of the province of Jersey, which must have become pretty numerous after a ten days invasion, unless indeed the Congress has entirely lost its credit and authority, and the people have learnt to distinguish their real enemies.

Secondly - Had the Comte ever been near to the detatchment that attacked and took entire possession of the quarters of the three companies that composed the infantry of his legion, he would have discovered that it did not amount to two hundred men, exclusive of fifty that remained a mile behind for the protection of the bridge, which the Comte so obligingly lent to them for a spare hour; or indeed had he or any of his surviving officers, amidst the variety of fireings, pursuits and military evolutions, in which it seems they were in a very secret manner employed that morning, approached within view either of their enemy's or of the boats in which they reimbarked, they would neither have deceived themselves nor their august masters in this manner.

Thirdly, had the Comte joined his infantry in any reasonable time, he must have added, that all their quarters were not only forced, but every officer and man in them cut off, except a few who escaped unarmed to conceal themselves in the neighbouring brakes, and some prisoners who, after the success of the attack was certain, were saved from the bayonnets of the soldiers.

The Comte pays no great compliments to his corps, when he says, that only two officers (out of nine that were with his infantry) stood to hazard their lives in trying to rally their men. In his next letter of amendments he ought in justice to inform you, that seven lost their lives on that occasion.

To save him the trouble of recollection the following are the names of five of them:
Lieutenant Colonel Bose, commanding the infantry.
Captain Fray, of the first company.
Captain Zecont of the second company.
Lieutenant Broderie, and
Lieutenant Stegs of the light-horse.

There were two other Lieutenants left for dead in their quarters, but the prisoners, altho' they knew the faces, did not recollect the names which were foreign.

And with regard to his loss in men, which it is humbly presumed amounts to two thirds of his infantry, you will be enabled to form a better idea of it, if you can prevail upon him to give in a return of the number of infantry now really existing in his corps. - Had the detachment been able to arrive at three o'clock, as the Comte supposes, it would possibly have found time to visit the stables, and to silence the fieldpiece with which he was amusing himself in firing alarm guns from time to time to solicit his neighbour Col. Proctor to his assistance. But the attack was not made till near five, and day opened whilst the British soldiers having no enemy before them, were ransacking the quarters of his late infantry. There is always on such occasions a moment before the officers can re-assemble their men, when a ready and enterprizing enemy may try what stuff their assailants are made of: But for such a purpose, there must be an officer capable of forming his plan instantly and executing it resolutely, followed by men fit for a close jostle in the dark. - Had the Comte and his horse been equal to such a task, his enemies would at least have had occasion to discharge their pieces, and would probably have had some men wounded, and possibly some killed before he was repulsed. As it was, the Comte will be pleased to allow that he had no occasion to hurt the wind of his horses in the pursuit, and that his enemies moved off with a gravity and leisure which could only be equalled by the modesty and respect with which they were followed. He will also allow that the rear guard, further to prevent unnecessary hurry and fatigue to his horses, halted repeatedly in a very open and sound ground, even before they reached the swamp and bridge which he with so much reason complains of; and he will further allow that they spent a full hour and a half in a retreat not exceeding two miles, so as to afford an opportunity for his cavalry of coming within random shot at least, without putting their horses to a trot, had they been so inclined.

In one respect however, to be candid, the Comte is right, his enemies did withdraw from him; yet whatever opinion he may have formed they certainly never meant to pass the season there, but only *to pay him a civil visit, and take their leave before they were introduced to too many of his neighbours; not that they had any objection to be accompanied a part of the way, in the very polite and respectful manner in which he knows so well to behave to - his friends.*

As I wish not entirely to engross a subject which may be so much better adorned by Comte Polaski's own illustrations, I shall leave for him the following queries.

At what pace did his horse pursue? did they ever approach near enough to exchange a shot?

What number did he kill? what number did he take, and how many wounded were left behind in the flight?

Whether the wicked tories (who must be bewitched, not to reclaim under so mild and free a government) have yet given up the five and twenty men whose retreat he cut off? for we are made to believe that there were only three men of the British detachment missing that night, one of whom, a deserter, has enlisted in the Continentals, another who it is presumed would rather smell strong if kept prisoner above ground, and a third, who possibly in the confusion of a night scramble may have lost himself, and remain the Compte's prisoner.

I have only to add that I am happy in affording Comte Polaski an opportunity of so easily refuting the assertions above mentioned, by producing the afore named officers of his legion said to be killed, and the wounded men and other made prisoners by him in the various actions he describes of that morning,

An officer who, in an unlucky or unguarded moment, should meet with a misfortune to affect his military character, although even exerting himself in a bad cause, will command the forbearance, if not the sympathy, of his adversaries, providing he apologizes for his conduct with modesty and candor; but if he should so far forget his situation as to assume a merit, and make a triumphant recital, founded on the grossest misrepresentation, concerning what a man

178

of reflection and feeling would naturally wish to have forgot, he has no farther claim to commiseration.
EGG-SHELL[89]

To Alexander Scrymgeour, 23 December 1778, New York:

New York Dec.[r] 23. 78.

My D:[r] Scrym.

In spite of Jack-nor-wester, who has taken obstinate possession of my ears nose, fingers & toes. altho in a room with a good fire, heres for you. My Arm, thank God, bids defiance to the frost, & Soul & Body are both very hearty & thriving - Sir H Clinton has given me some thing ado for the present - by appointing me dry-nurse to 150 of the 71st who have been Prisoners in new England - To this he was pleased to give the name of a Command; however as these men as soon as fit for Service will join their regiment in Georgia I know the difference, however, fit for Service they shall be. His excellency had another Command in view for me & I understood myself certain of it, but have met with a heavy disappointment. [His] design was to form all the men belonging to Burgoigne who had escaped from the [page torn] a Corps for your humble Servant. As their fidelity was individually proved, & as they would be extremely inveterate & could not look for Quarter & as they were moreover made Soldiers, the man who had them must have got reputation. but it was afterwards determined to disperse them through the army. - I mean not to complain of my usage, for I beleive Sir H. C. means me very well: & I know he has it in view to give me the first Majority - he has repeatedly said so, & I have thorough confidence in his word - but there is Little Chance.

however, I must next Campaign & then farewell all further promotion to a [ink blot - man without a] farthing & who has been the unfortunate instrument of inquiring the Circumstances of his freinds.

I inclose you two Essays I publish'd in the Papers here. Those [un]der the Signature of Momento mori have met with the approbation of the Public. John Bull I meant as a counterpoize to American vanity & insolence. If your newspapers will print them it will give them another week of Existence.

God Bless you all & beleive me most affectionately yours.

[Note above by Betty Scrymgeour: New York 23ᵈ Decʳ 1778][90]

"To the Author of CRISIS, No. VI", by 'Memento Mori' (Patrick Ferguson), publ. in *The Royal Gazette* (James Rivington, New York), No. 223, Wednesday 18 November 1778, p. 2.

[In Patrick's hand, two copies:]

Nᴼ. 1.]

To the Author of CRISIS, No. VI

THERE is a simplicity in the unadorned language of virtue and reason, never to be found in the florid stile and turgid periods of faction and treason. In the one the address is made to the understanding, and to those benevolent affections that tend to the happiness and elevation of man. In the other, truth and nature are perverted, the malevolent passions excited and every sentence loaded with rancorous and indecent epithets, that to an unprejudiced and well conditioned mind prove their own antidote.

To which of these descriptions apply the late Manifesto of the Commissioners, and to which that paper you have opposed to it; will be determined in due time, by their effect upon the minds of the people. Had I the honour of your correspondence, I should expect to be told in a language intirely free from insult, coarse abuse, affected triumph, and idle declamation, that "you with confidence rest your cause upon the event" AND THERE SIR, LET IT REST.

But remember that the delusion is near at an end: that the people have had some experience of the blessings. of your government, that they have had full time to compare the share of personal freedom, security of property, general protection, and more particularly that exemption from taxation which they have hitherto enjoyed, and have so fair a future prospect of, under the auspices of the Congress, to the grievances they formerly experienced when in union with their mother country, and to those severe and equivocal terms now held out to their acceptance. Remember too, that passion and prejudice at length subside, that men by degrees learn from experience, if not from reflection to discover how far the pursuits of their rulers coincide with the interests of the society. - How far they are influenced by motives of private emolument and ambition, or governed by a true patriotism founded on the love of general freedom, justice and humanity.

Consider that men will, and can count, and that the majority of the freemen of America, who are now excluded from the common privilege they all heretofore enjoyed, of voting at the election of their representatives, must have become sensible of the advantages of that policy which relieves them from so troublesome a task, particularly at a time when taxes are so equally and sparingly imposed and justice so truly and mildly administered, and consequently that they must be ready to hazard their lives and fortunes, with alacrity, in support of their new modelled government.

Consider how probable it is that the Congress, citizens of the world, and philosophers as they all are themselves, should prevail upon colonies of Englishmen to forget all the narrow impolitic prejudices, and idle affections, founded on consanguinity, and on the habits of long union, friendship and intercourse, and to concur heartily with the King of France, that renowned protector of the rights of mankind, in an attempt to overwhelm Great-Britain, the noted enemy of liberty.

Consider again what confidence the inhabitants of America must have in the disinterested views of the Congress, not only from the great stock of original property that those members. who most strenuously oppose a reconciliation, hazard in the contest, as well as from the personal danger they expose themselves to in the field, but also from the known characters of those gentlemen - so distinguished for probity, so void of ambition, so averse to rule, so fond of peace and order, of justice and humanity.

Consider all. these things, and then LOOK WELL TO YOURSELVES. - Your political pursuits do indeed equal honour to the soundness of your hearts and of your heads. - When virtue and wisdom unite, who can doubt the event!

I have the more willingly indulged the effusions of my mind in this tribute of gratitude so justly due to the dignified legislators of this new world, that I might also confirm your confidence which appears to me in this your last paper to be rather assumed, notwithstanding the fire and elegance of your composition, and the depth and soundness of your reasoning.

Fear not my friend - Reflect that you are the champion chosen by the Congress to undermine the specious arguments and offers of the British Commissioners, to sap by degrees those idle impressions that, both from nature and education still weigh with the weak part of the Americans, and to prepare them for the new principles of policy and morals which Messrs. Adams have so happily introduced.

Reflect that, until the minds of men are totally changed, the Congress cannot openly combat their prejudices, without incurring general odium; that therefore they have wisely resolved to avoid all argument with the British Commissioners on the various subjects addressed to them; and that through your efforts, and the efforts of men like you alone, can the minds of the people be stored with the philosophy necessary to make them sensible of the happiness their governors are preparing for them.

A the Old Baily in England, (where it is still the practice as it was once with us, for men to be condemned to death for taking away the property or lives of others without just cause as warranted by established precedent of law, and for conspiring against the constitution of their country) it is a custom with the Newgate solicitors to prepare the pannels for their defence by previously personating the council that prosecute, and urging all the arguments and questions that might be offered at the Bar against their clients: - ---- Altho' in most things the usages as well as the manners and principles of the French are become much more to my taste than those of England, I confess I think this a wise custom, and I shall therefore, if you please, so far force my nature as to personate a loyalist in the remaining part of this letter, and argue accordingly.

In the Crisis you are pleased to compare the British nation to devils, whose canine venom and unheard of cruelties imported from the original warehouse of Hell, have during the course of this war, exceeded the savages of either Indies. - You say that the proposals of the Royal Commissioners are horrid and infernal, the union of madness and absurdity, Bedlam in concert with Lucifer - You threaten retaliation; to burn every house, manufacture and ship in England, to trepan our army and to give no sort of quarter, (God preserve us) and conclude, that the time may come when Britain shall in vain sue for peace from France and her American allies." - These, if I mistake not, are your words - I wish not to add to their energy - they are new - in print at least, and need no embellishment, either as to sense, sentiment or language - However, we cannot help thinking them a little too severe.

Had it been the inclination of Great Britain, to pursue the most short, easy and certain method of putting an end to the rebellion, without regard to the sufferings of her unhappy colonists, her armies, having been in possession of most of the capital towns of America, might certainly have burnt them to the foundation, and have laid in ruin and desolation the most flourishing provinces without expence or trouble, or without going one foot out of their way, had not the Generals restrained the just indignation of the soldiers, who, enraged at the severities and cruelties exercised against the loyalists, at the very base and ungallant mode of war generally employed by the rebels, and at the particular treachery and duplicity of that part of the peasantry that took arms against them, have been with difficulty witheld from doing justice to themselves and their country.

The British soldier, allowed by all mankind, except his rebel relations, to be as generous as brave, has been ever the most ready to receive with open arms that enemy which best tried his metal in the fair contentions of the field for glory; and if in any instances he should appear to have lost the native generosity of his disposition, the world, who know his character, will enquire into the provocation before he is condemned. - Should he be accused of having refused to give quarter, the most christian soldier will acquit him when he is told the enemy he put to death, in place of meeting him fairly in action, made it a practice to fire at him and fly, from fence to fence, until he was disabled from doing more mischief by being overtaken; or had wounded him as soon as his back was turned from the very house; at the threshold of which, he had met him with open arms, made professions of loyalty, and received his protection. Every soldier must smile to hear a party at war complain of breach of the peace, and reproach their antagonists because in a night attack they did not previously awake their enemies, warn them of their danger, and give them the choice of defending themselves with advantage, or of running away. Complaints of this kind betray an extreme effeminacy of spirit, and a natural incapacity for the rough struggles of serious service.

One would imagine that you had with your usual modesty proposed, and that Great-Britain, with her wonted good nature had agreed, that you should fire at her troops whenever you pleased, and run off, and that when they caught you they were to make much of you; that you should for your amusement break their bones from your windows, and that in return, they should protect your persons and place safeguards at your doors; that you should hang round their camp, desolate your own country to cramp their subsistance, and take every opportunity of committing safe murder, and that they in return should watch over your slumbers, and procure to your detachments quiet and safe dreams.

But the British troops relish not the christian meekness and forbearance that have prevailed so much in the councils at home. They have in mind your treatment of General Burgoyne's troops with difficulty prevailed upon to prefer your faith to a death by famine. They know you, and fear your smiles more than your enmity. What they give they are ready to take, and as they are ever disposed to respect and do justice to real gallantry, even in the persons of rebels, so will they do strict justice upon those skulking assassins who disgrace and degrade the profession of arms.

You also endeavour to charge the British army with the injuries that the country is necessarily exposed to from being the seat of war. Hitherto sheltered under the parental wings of England, little do the Americans know the unavoidable distress and ruin that follow the footsteps of the best disciplined armies.

In Hanover, the favourite territory of the late King, the crop of grain when green was annually consumed as forage by the army assembles there last war for its defence; the fences and wood used as fire by the troops; garden stuff and fruit taken without any restriction by the men; and no sort of compensation made for any of these articles to the inhabitants - nor for the poultrey, cattle and houses that the soldiers will find means to plunder at times in spite of all restraint: -

Moreover the farmers were made to drive to the magazines of the army at a stated price, what remains of storage and grain they had saved during harvest for their winter's provision; and those who did no comply were necessarily treated as enemies, their produce taken by force, and not paid for, and contributions raised upon them, under penalty of burning their houses, and laying waste the country, if they resisted or refused. Much of this have the unhappy inhabitants of this continent experienced from their own troops, with this cruel aggravation, that what they are paid for is in counters, and that they are insulted and plundered under pretence of protecting their liberty and property; - much more must they necessarily experience from both armies, in the future progress of the war, if they are prevailed upon to sacrifice their private security, rights and happiness in a vain attempt to erect an untimely throne for their seducers. MEMENTO MORI.

[To be concluded on Saturday.][91]

Part Two of 'Memento Mori' (Patrick Ferguson), *The Royal Gazette*, No. 224, Saturday 21 November 1778, p. 3

[In Patrick's hand:

[Nº. 2.]

Continuation of the Piece signed MEMENTO MORI, inserted in last Wednesday's Paper.

THOSE Americans who are not sufficiently cured of their passion for prosecuting a war without an object by the preceding account of the unavoidable hardships that they will necessarily suffer from the army the most disposed to favour then, I shall refer to the attested accounts of the ravages of their French allies in Hanover last war, and in the different provinces of Germany during the invasions of Louis the XIV. The outrages there committed against persons of all sexes and conditions, and the unheard of indignities offered to the Protestant Churches and worship, will not be read without indignation and horror by all who are endued with a love. of liberty, humanity and religion, unless indeed they are initiated in the new philosophy.

That the country has suffered by the British army no man will deny with any success, unless he can prove that it was not composed of men like other armies, but of angels: But let it be remembered that the officers could not hazard to disgust the men, who were uncommonly irritated from the nature of the war, by the restraints of a very rigid discipline without assisting the views of the rebels, who applied themselves most assiduously to profit by the opportunities that their connections and the same language afforded of promoting desertion; and that the troops were obliged to help themselves and take what they could, as they were not only prevented from supplying their wants by fair purchase, by the unjust and severe punishments inflicted by the rebel officers and committees on such of the inhabitants as approached the British camp to receive payment for the cattle which the detachments had been under a necessity of collecting, but also as the Congress adopted the policy equally ruinous, dastardly and cruel, of laying waste the country they professed to protect, in order to throw a momentary inconvenience in the way of an enemy whom they durst not openly oppose.

The rebel chiefs are therefore alone answerable for the irregularities which they have forced the British troops to practice, as well as for the injuries the country has sustained from the necessities and licentiousness of their own. The balance against them is not forgot, and AT THE SETTLEMENT OF ACCOUNTS WILL BE DULY STATED.

Had the British nation or officers suffered the just resentment of the soldiers to have had way, Boston and Philadelphia, Newcastle, Wilmington, Chester, Germantown, Bristol, Burlington, Trenton, Princetown, Brunswick, Elizabeth-town, Amboy, New-Ark and many other towns, with the best parts of the provinces of New-York, Pennsylvania, and New-Jersey would not have had, at this time, a house remaining to receive an inhabitant. Mr. Washington, in a public letter has done justice to Sir William Howe with regard to the state in which Boston was left; and every inhabitant of Philadelphia must remember that Sir Henry Clinton put his army to the inconvenience of laying upon the ground the night before he quitted that town, to prevent its being plundered or burnt; for which last purpose one lighted straw, privately applied, is sufficient among wooden buildings, such as generally prevail in America.

Thus had it been the design either of the British officers or of the Generals or of the nation to have connived at, much less to have encouraged, the irregularities of the soldiers, the war would now have been at an end, and America disabled from disturbing the peace of the world for at least a century to come. But this is a trifle to what the Congress lay to their charge. They boldly and roundly assert without hesitation or circumlocution, that the King's forces have been employed during this war of express purpose in desolating the country and burning the towns to the utmost of their power, in imitation, I presume, of their own policy at New-York, when chased from it. If I may venture, without incurring ridicule, to enter into a refutation of an assertion so palpably extravagant, I would observe, that the army, had this been its object, would not have been much retarded on its way to Elk Head, in demolishing Norfolk, Williamsburg, Baltimore and Annapolis with the settlements around; and as Mr. Washington, with the whole Continental army nearly, joined to the militia of the populous provinces of Jersey and Pennsylvania, and assisted by the presence of the Congress, could not prevent the British troops, altho' deprived of all communication with their ships, from penetrating into the heart of America, possessing themselves of Philadelphia, (prepared for defence at an

*expence in forts, gallies, chevaux de frize, & c. which they can
scarce again afford to repeat) and chasing those sages a little
irreverently from their stools, it will not be pretended that the feeble
provinces of Virginia and Maryland could have covered their towns,
open as they are, close to the water, and made up of combustibles,
against the united exertions of the British fleet and army: And had
the army afterwards burnt Philadelphia, (in place of losing a
campaign in covering that town, and in unavailing attempts to
reclaim the rebel by mild means,) directed its avenging steps to the
south, and revisited New-England and the other provinces at the
opposite extremity with the returning Sun, WHAT, O AMERICA
WOULD NOW BE YOUR CONDITION! - May your rulers never
force you from experience to know how much more easily you are to
be compelled to your duty by 5000 men employed in serious
hostilities, than win to your interest by a mock war carried on by
50,000.*

*The tone of insult, defiance and exaltation affected by the
Congress, cannot surely so totally blind you, but that you must be
sensible that the force necessary to occupy any one of your towns,
will prove more than sufficient to burn to the ground in one summer
almost every sea port and town upon the continent.*

*Compare your numbers, resources, military force and extent
of frontier to that of France, and recall to your minds the last war,
when that powerful kingdom could not protect about an hundred
leagues of coast laying upon the English Channel, (the principal and
professed object of our expeditions,) with an army of 300,000
standing forces; joined to twice as many militia; (for there were ten
millions of inhabitants within 100 leagues of the points attacked,)
every where provided with numerous artillery and warlike stores;
with the advantage of a fighting cavalry; thrice as numerous as the
Continental army; and capable of pushing with great expedition
from one extremity to the other of the frontier threatened; the whole
coast covered with fortresses, each of which able to withstand for
months an attack from a well provided army of 50,000 men; - and
the country to at man united under an established government in one
common cause.*

The force employed in these expeditions did not much exceed in numbers, either of the corps now stationed at Rhode Island or Halifax, or one half of the army lying idle in the environs of New-York; and yet they not only invaded the open towns and country at pleasure, but took and demolished the strong fortress and important harbour of Cherburgh, burnt the French ships under the very cannon of St. Maloes, and kept the whole coast in constant alarm.

What then will hyperbole and impotent bravadoes avail the rebels of America, should Great-Britain be unhappily forced to disable where she cannot reclaim, and in her own defence be necessitated to destroy, in a few months, those settlements that have cost her ages of parental attention and unmerited generosity to rear.

Had your usurpation the sanction of a long establishment, had it been founded on necessity, and maintained with a due regard to freedom and justice, even with respect to your own society, in place, of being a treasonable conspiracy of a few artful feigned enthusiasts to gain an unlimited command of the lives and properties of their fellow-subjects, by fanning the sacred fire of liberty to a flame that ever is sure to consume the materials of which it is composed - Were you even to a man united, in place of having in the bosom of every Province a great proportion of spirits smarting under the weight of heavy and recent injuries) who detest your tyranny and wait with impatience for an opportunity of spurning you from your mock-throne - how could you hope to defend yourselves?

Your numbers little exceeding two millions, and these a motley mixture of unresisting quakers, disaffected slaves, sickly enervated planters in the south, and ungovernable republicans in the north, all encumbered with families and an uncommon proportion of helpless children, scattered over a tract of country 1200 miles in extent in a direct line, and having 1800 miles of coast to cover, including the different indents that every where enable a naval force to find shelter from the storms unmolested from the shore, to enter into the heart of the country, interrupt all communication, disembark and reimbark in smooth water, almost every where and at all seasons; and elude the preparations against it by throwing itself at choice on the side undefended.

Your whole standing army (in spite of all the oppressive means employed to force men into your service, in spite of the immense public debt incurred, as well as of the private loss every where to individuals by having their cattle, grain and clothing forced from them at an half and a third of the current price, to feed and clothe your starving soldiers and needy French allies) not equal to one of several detachments that could to-morrow be let loose upon your coast: And composed mostly of Irish and Germans who despise you, and who could without any expence to Government be easily induced by an offer of a part of that property which you have forfeited to the laws of your country, to strip you of your borrowed plumes and leave you to the indignation of your enemies and contempt of the world.

Your country without one walled town, and the united exertion of your whole continent unequal to furnish the materials, artificers and labourers necessary to build one good fortress, such as there are hundreds on the frontiers of France and Germany; and which are absolutely essential to the existence, not to say the security of a people, however numerous, collected and powerful in other respects, who pretend to make war without having a superior naval force to protect their coast.

Moreover the very extent, divided and unfortified situation of the American settlements that have increased the difficulties of reducing them and keeping them to their duty by gentle means, where the first object was to save the country and spare the inhabitants, will render it easy at least in the same proportion, when serious offensive measures are adopted to disable and extinguish the whole force of the Provinces in detail. - The mystery of our want of success will then be at an end, and PROMPT CONVICTION FOLLOW THE EXPERIMENT. - In the mean time weigh these circumstances well and EXULT IN YOUR STRENGTH.

To trace the various hesitating and reluctant steps with which Great-Britain has been urged by encreasing provocation to proceed to extremities against her rebel colonists, must excite in every mind susceptible of virtuous impressions, a mixture of affection, veneration and regret - and will furnish in future history

190

some of the brightest pages to adorn the annals of man. Posterity will there see a powerful nation, doubtful of the strict justice of the claims of her ministers, and respecting the errors of liberty even to the extremes of licence and disorder, with difficulty prevailed upon to use the mildest coercive measures in support of that authority of government, essential to the existence of mankind in society; a large proportion both of the people and of their representatives contending. for concessions in favour of the revolted provinces, in spite of the indignity and extreme impolicy of yielding to armed subjects; the nation submitting to continued expence, and offering terms infinitely beyond the original claims of the insurgents, and her troops at the same time foregoing every where the fruits of those successes which they owed to their superior virtue, rather than oppress, by the usual modes of enforcing submission, a people whom they believed to be deluded.

So far will posterity respect the illustrious self denial and forbearance of England; but when it shall be recorded that the rebel cabal broke the most solemn conventions, employed secret emissaries to burn her fleets and docks, prevailed upon her most formidable enemies to join with them in times of full peace in conspiring her ruin, and rejected with the strongest marks of inveteracy and insult, every practical proffer of an equal union and alliance; piety, justice and all the charities will join to applaud the vengeance, however severe, that shall follow, providing it is levelled at the guilty alone, and that the public atone for any unhappy mistakes that may be made.

There are who assert the impossibility of discriminating, and from thence infer the necessity of involving the provinces in one general undistinguished ruin. - But the generous spirit of Englishmen will ever revolt at an idea which the extreme necessity of self-preservation can alone justify, - For the present, policy equally with justice and humanity forbid it. The means to avoid the innocent is very simple, and 50,000 l would more than compensate the mistakes of two years ravages; and thus signal and strict justice be executed on those who have been active and continue obstinate in rebellion; indulgence extended to all who have involuntarily been obliged to submit to the tyranny, and co-operate with the views of their seditious demagogues; and the forfeitures would be more than

sufficient to indemnify those subjects who adhere to their allegiance, as well as to reward those who, with a bolder virtue, hazard their lives in support of the constitution of their country.
MEMENTO MORI.[92]

Part Three of 'Memento Mori' (Patrick Ferguson), *The Royal Gazette*, no. 232, Saturday 19 December 1778, p. 3

[In Patrick's hand:

N⁰. 3.]

MEMENTO MORI. No. 3.
TO know that my former letters have drawn the attention, and been honoured by the approbation of many thinking men amongst the officers of the army and navy, as well as amongst the loyalists assembled here from the different provinces of America, neither excites in me emotions of vanity or surprize, as I believe myself possessed of common sense, and am conscious of an honest meaning. For the subject, to those divested of passion & prejudice, and who have an opportunity of judging upon the spot, is easily understood, requiring no uncommon powers of genius or of language.

Neither shall I be surprized when I am informed, as I shall in due time, that these essays have been favoured with still a more attentive and serious perusal, by that illustrious assemblage of self proclaimed and of self denying patriots, who, not contented with the success of their former endeavours, are still most piously employed at Philadelphia in inventing new ways and means of encreasing the happiness and adding to the virtue of their disciples; and who with a modesty peculiar to themselves, not only discourage and stifle all those free discussions of their merits and services, that would otherwise naturally find their way into the public prints of the United States (where the utmost freedom of the press must of course be allowed by those champions of liberty, as essential to its existence) but also most assiduously intercept and conceal those complimentary essays wrote out of their jurisdiction, by men whose praise must redound still more to the glory of the Congress, as they have nothing to hope for or expect from it. Among these I beg to be ranked, and flatter myself that I shall be able to furnish some new ideas not only to W. H. Drayton and the other ostensible parts of that machine which Messieurs Adams are pleased to play upon so much to the edification as well as the advantage of their fortunate admirers, but even to introduce some new images and subjects of serious contemplation to the mind of Sam. Adams himself. In my last essay I enumerated some of those weaknesses that put it out of the power of the British Colonies to stand their ground in a state of independence, however much they may be inclined from vanity, levity, want of principle, character or foresight; or any other vicious propensity to aim at, or rather indeed to ape a condition which they are utterly unequal to support and maintain; but least an overdose on that copious subject might have operated with a violence and delirium generally occasioned by the rash prescriptions of the Congress, I have reserved a few ingredients which I mean to administer by way of alterative in this, and in another paper.

Having already shewn that the frontier of the truly free and independent States of North America towards the sea, is so equally open to invasion and ruin throughout its whole extent, that happily no particular province can have reason to be more apprehensive than another; it remains to examine whether the security which the Congress is pleased to proclaim and promise to the inhabitants with an air of infallibility and a sublimity of language peculiar to themselves and to Chrononhotonthologos alone, is equally well founded with regard to the back frontier, which is fully as extensive and much more thinly peopled than the other.

The Indians whom they have there to cope with, (having remarked the fatal consequences that Generals Carleton and Burgoyne experienced by restraining them from pursuing their own mode of war, and being in other respects little inclined to follow our example in complying with all the stipulations of their enemies, relative to the kind of war and the degree of severity which it will be the least disagreeable and inconvenient for them to be exposed to,) have to the Northward seriously taken up the hatchet against them, reserving their smiles for their friends alone. And altho' unsupported by Great-Britain, they, together with the unhappy loyalists (who *have been chased, by the heavy and unrelenting hand of oppression, from all the blessings of domestic life and comforts of civilized society, to partake amongst the rude inhabitants of the wilderness of that liberty which was refused them at home,) have already demonstrated so closely to the feelings of the inhabitants in various quarters throughout the northern provinces, how very much that frontier is open to desolation and destruction, that little requires to be said, * I shall therefore only observe, that if the more numerous southern nations of Indians, who only wait for the word, were allowed and encouraged to act upon the back of Maryland, Virginia, and the Carolinas, in concert with their northern brethren; their operations alone reinforced as they would be from the loyalists, impatient for the recovery of constitutional liberty, and of their just rights as freemen, would fully employ all the wisdom, power and resources of the rebel confederacy. - These warriors have some customs equally shocking to the humanity of Congress and to the delicacy of the continental troops. For they not only subsist themselves without ceremony at the expence of their enemies, but they lay waste without scruple, those tracts of country on their frontier that might otherwise enable the rebels to establish and keep up posts in their neighbourhood to act against them; and when their enemies fly, after having done all the mischief in their power, they not only adopt the unfair and savage custom of pursuing them with perseverence, but generally when they overtake them, do, as they would be done by, and endeavour by drawing a steady and marked line between their conduct to them and their friends, to command respect, good faith and awe from the one, and secure the love and attachment of the other, equally regardless of the complaints, remonstrances and pious ejaculations of the Congress & of their friends, to the feelings of all of whom this mode of procedure is as unpleasant, as it is inconvenient to their affairs. - They are extremely irregular too in their ways, paying little attention to the American etiquette of time and place - day or night, Saturday or Sunday, it is all one to them - never announce themselves either, but tumble in pell mell. And what is worse than all, they have no faith in continental promises or conventions - and very little taste for those heroic and elegant compositions which have been so much the wonder and admiration of the rest of the world.*

If during last war the whole force of British America, united to a man, in a common cause (whilst the mother country armed, paid and fed their soldiers, assisted them with a body of troops exceeding in numbers the whole force they could themselves furnish, and twice as numerous as the present Continental army, supplied at the same time all their wants as to money, arms, warlike engines and stores, and protected their whole coast with her triumphant navy) were for four years engaged in a hard struggle against only a part of the Indians, seconded by a very few thousand French and Canadians, before the scales were so far turned that they durst at any time pronounce themselves secure for three months from being vanquished and enslaved; what have they now to expect, when the Indians (who seem to retain a thorough sense of the humility and good offices they have experienced from them) are ready throughout the Continent to strike; seconded by number of indignant Colonies who have felt the oppression and observed the various weak parts of the rebel states - ready too to be supported at the same time from the Floridas, back forts and lakes, Canada and Nova Scotia, by a much larger body of regular troops than the French could ever detach for offensive operations in the days of American dismay and prostration, without exposing their main settlements upon the river St. Lawrence; and when instead of commanding the arms, marine and resources of Great Britain, the forces and fleets of that kingdom only wait for orders to spread the miseries of real war along the open indefensible tracts of settlements near to the sea, which comprehend above one half of the population and wealth, & the whole of the shipping and trade of America; whilst the Indians embrace the still more defenceless back frontier, and involve the provinces in the horrors of unceasing desolation and irremediable ruin.

So far have the republicans of America reason to boast of their security and independence without - many of their weaknesses within have been pointed out in a former paper. - As the catalogue is long, and several of them are singly decisive against the success of their resistance, I may be excused for having then omitted those that follow:

Th extreme corruption that prevails among those who have assumed the government of their affairs, must of itself, without any concurring causes, soon work their ruin. For the truth of the fact I would appeal were it necessary to the letters of Mifflin, Lee, and of the patriotic incendiary Silas Deane; but there is even better proof than this reciprocal self-accusations of the parties.† For the immense quantities of paper money that have been avowedly issued under pretence of defraying public expences, when compared with the small number¶ and scanty pay of the rebel standing army, with the very low and unfair price which the farmers and other inhabitants have been obliged to receive for the produce, clothing and manufactures, forced from them under pretence of supplying the wants of the soldiers, and with the very trifling expence of their petit-aigre marine and other visible disbursements, sufficiently proclaim the excessive embezzlements and frauds that have everywhere prevailed in the management of their funds; and the amount of the sums that they have already to liquidate by taxing themselves, may enable them to form some idea of the future expence of a war, which from the nature of the alliance formed by the Congress, must become inveterate as well as obstinate, and of long duration - Indeed this was a natural consequence of the American commotions, and every man in any degree versant in history, or acquainted with human nature, could have foretold, had it been possible for reason to gain a hearing from the tools of blind enthusiasm and passion, that a new settled and extensive country, which had received with its first settlers those habits of luxury, avarice and corruption, (that are scarce to be counteracted, in the more powerful compact and long established governments of Europe, by the various checks from time to time devised and gradually introduced as the evils arise,) and that had abandoned itself from its very infancy in an inordinate degree to commerce, and its attendant an unbounded thirst of lucre, should be able to avoid bankruptcy and the extremes of civil commotion, even if left to itself, amidst the various fields for avarice and ambition that would open to the inexperience of the people - much less to assume that degree of disinterested patriotism, regardless of riches, safety, power, pleasure or ease, necessary to enable them to make head against the serious trials that are preparing for them. Indeed that perfection of Roman virtue which the Congress and their cabal with so much gravity and becoming dignity put in an exclusive claim for, and which in fact alone could enable them to stand their ground, has not hitherto ever prevailed in this world among extensive or numerous societies, and has been entirely confined to small communities, uncorrupted by luxury, unseduced by a passion for riches, ignorant of the refinements now termed civilization, but nurtured in danger and hardship, and their minds from infancy made to look forward to the public weal, regardless of all personal feelings and considerations; whilst their actions held forth to general view in the narrow but magnifying focus of a small community, afforded no escape from infamy by shifting their ground to take shelter with such men as our modern citizens of the world.

As to the Americans it is well if they preserve the virtues permitted to their situation - honesty in private dealings, obedience to lawful authority and humanity. The sterner and more exalted ones of heroism, and disinterested patriotism, of which we read in ancient story, are composed of tougher and purer materials, and wove of a closer texture in a more firm and compact loom. There are to be sure, some illustrious modern exceptions - Some men, who, in spite of the effeminacy and selfishness of our education, regardless of the wealth so generally sought after and respected in the world, above being tempted by the trophies of power, or the bewitching blandishments of popular applause, are superior to pleasure and dissipation, have regarded with a steady and empassioned eye, and advanced with a firm unremitting step upon the sacred models of antiquity: But it is not probable that a number of attornies, smuggling traders, slave-driving planters, hatters, carpenters and the like, should throughout an extent of 1500 miles, start up by one consent heroes in grain, and by sudden inspiration, mount from their superior virtue to the head of society with the most disinterested views, forgetful of the dissipated and lewd habits, sordid pursuits and fraudulent practices of their former lives. The Congress would therefore do well to give some proof of their regeneration to the unbelieving world, before they hold forth in tragedy strains in favour of their unnatural transformation.
MEMENTO MORI

* Vide Governor Clinton's speech and the answer of the rebel Assembly at Poughkeepsie, Colonel Butler's and Parker's account of the Indian expeditions, and those others in the rebel

papers describing the progress of the Indians at Wyoming, the German Flats, Cherry Valley, & c.

    † *In the Pennsylvania Ledger of the 18th of March 1778, and in the Pennsylvania Pacquet of the 28th March, 1778, it is proved by a writer under the signature of Pacificus, from the resolves and vouchers produced by the Congress, that the debts then contracted by the United States and publicly avowed by their treasurers, amounted to fifty millions, six hundred, and twenty five thousand pounds Pennsylvania Currency, exclusive of interest; and as this year must have added considerably to the score, the inhabitants would do well to estimate the expence of feeding our army and their Indian friends (who will probably help themselves in future) before they fall in with the proposals of Governor Clinton at Poughkeepsie, and their other rulers, to tax themselves with a view to liquidate these trifling sums.*

    ¶ *Possibly the rebels may say they are now more numerous - it may be in women and children perhaps, but let them count the immense loss of men in their Canadian expeditions, in their repeated defeats, and in general in their army, from want of stamina and discipline, together with the loss for several years, of the emigrations of hardy Europeans, from the former supplies of whom, they have both recruited their army, mann'd their privateers and carried on the necessary manufactures.*[93]

Satire "To the Inhabitants of the Thirteen United States of America", by "John Bull" (Patrick Ferguson), publ. in *The Royal Gazette*, New York, No. 231, Wed. 16 December 1778, p. 2

    To the Inhabitants of the Thirteen United States of America

    O YE demi gods of this western hemisphere! If a being, born and bred in the impure and enfeebling regions of Europe, dare look up to the radiant glories that glow around your heads, listen, O listen to a mortal voice!

    Elegant as you are in your manners! elevated in your sentiments! accomplished in every personal attainment! and your souls expanding at each pulsation of your hearts with an ardent thirst of glory and honour, attemper'd by sweet humanity and sober justice - you miracles of nature all hail!

Freedom, the arts and every virtue you well affect, follow the course of the Sun. - On the bosom of the liberal air does liberty approach your coasts in every eastern gale: The swelling Atlantic with every tide heaves a new art upon your shores: The virtues mounted on sun-beams abandon Europe, to pour their blessings with every meridian ray upon your selected heads. Chosen spirits, all hail! heroes incog, we bow before you!

To our mortal eyes did you appear an inferior breed of man, neither equal to the sons of Europe in vigor of mind nor in personal hardiness. - Struggling under the languors of a sickning perpendicular sun, or frozen with seeming torpor and stupefaction in your winter dens, you have ever excited our commiseration, but never awakened our envy. - Scarce ever mature, and that which for want of better you call'd your prime of life, of so languid a complexion and short a duration, that we could not, until thus enlighten'd, easily draw the line between your manhood and your dotage. Caution, distrust, and timid prudence, the usual concomitants of age, usurping upon better feelings and generous passions peculiar in other climates to youth; and the severe characters of time, that, with premature strides took early possession of your countenances, seemed to warn the spectator of the unseasonable change within - Your bodies in general corresponding with the character of your minds, slender and pliant, without any of those masculine marks of breadth of chest, swelling muscles, or sanguine complexion that enable manly and determined spirits to act up to their bent, and that confirm and encrease the confidence of all others. We observed that nature had given to the fierce but unsuspicious bull and to other animals of the same character a broad chest and short but strong limbs - To the fearful deer and others of his cast watchfulness and long legs. To the men of Europe, shoulders, muscles and a redundancy of blood. To you - uncommon length of limbs and a sickly helpless aspect. - We allowed however for your disadvantages - We had known you from time to time to display some of those qualities that proclaimed your progenitors and

199

looked forward with confidence to the future effects of blood and example, however unfavourable the clime. We knew that virtue was within reach of all men, and though it might alter a little with the temper and constitution, we were prepared to adore the goddess in whatever garb she appeared, and to embrace her followers: Indeed she is never so respectable as when rising superior to natural infirmity; and we had therefore a double portion of esteem and affection ready for those Americans who strove for the palm.

When we saw numbers unseduced by the arts of sedition, unmoved by the frenzy of an intemperate enthusiasm, regardless of their property and personal safety, adhere to their duty; and conscious of the true interests of America, cherish in their bosoms those feelings of loyalty to the King and constitution, and of social affection and attachments to their relations and fellow subjects in Europe, which had been heretofore so much the means of our mutual happiness and prosperity, we reverenced the examples of superior virtue held out to us by our American kinsmen. But how much alas have we and they been deceived. Blessed be the age in which an Adams, a Franklin and a Congress have been produced, to disclose to the wondering world so new and exalted a system of policy and of morals.

Emanations of virtue and wisdom, pardon, 0 pardon our errors. Without those calls to honour and merit to be derived from the excitements of ancestry, national character, the habits of honour, and the prospects of those distinguishing allurements to glorious emulation, that are incompatible with your republican levelling principles, how much does your superior excellence astonish the world!

We, in our ignorance, were made to believe that Europe owed its ascendancy among mankind to singular advantages in point of climate and situation. We imagined that its soil in proportion to its extent was the most fertile on the globe; and that fertility much enhanced by being every where so near the sea, as to be able to throw its produce into the circulation of commerce, so as at the same time to favour population, agriculture, and manufactures, and turn its riches to account, - that the climate was temperate and pure, not only from the zone in which it was placed, and from long clearing and cultivation, but also from the peculiar salubrity and temperature derived from those two great arms of salt water, the Baltic and the Mediterranean, that forbid the approach of putrefaction, disarm the winter of its frost, and soften the deadly fury of the summer's sun. We had observed that no part of the known world that was two hundred leagues from the sea, had ever been inhabited in any degree, however fertile the soil and happy the clime. Throughout almost the whole extent of Siberia and Tartary in Asia, as well as throughout the interior parts of Africa and of North and South-America, there never has been science, arts or power, or indeed men in sufficient numbers to deserve the name of a people - a few wandering savages indeed, who only prove that mankind can neither domesticate nor multiply in those regions.

Hence we believed that Europe, having a large proportion, and indeed quantity, of land really habitable, and capable of receiving a numerous and civilised people than is any where else to be met with within the temperate zones, and possessing the various advantages above enumerated, would undoubtedly continue to reign triumphant Queen of the World, until God should please to alter the laws by which heretofore the universe had been governed.

We observed, that in hot latitudes, the human judgment was weak, the mind irresolute, and the imagination precipitate: that in the opposite extremes, the powers of the mind were indolent, the apprehension slow, and genius torpid, - and blessed heaven for having placed us in the golden mean; bowing with gratitude to the power that had thrown us into that garden where the human plant has grown with the most vigour, pre-eminent in science and virtue, rising as of a different race above the rest of mankind in intelligence, in exertion, in courage, in humanity.

If Europe appeared to us to possess extensive advantages over the other quarters of the globe, the British Islands seemed to enjoy others still superior. There the inhabitants protected during the summer by a curtain thrown by the favouring hand of nature between them and the sun, to shade them from the madning as well as enfeebling effects of his meredian beams, enjoy the full powers of an healthy imagination and sound judgement in vigorous body, at a time when the rest of the world are overcome with indolence and relaxation, and their brains affected by the distempered mid day sun. - There too, shielded in winter by the surrounding ocean, the soil unbound by the frost is open to cultivation, and the general air mild enough to allow every man to follow his employment and enjoy society at large, whilst in other climes the elements are fixed in irresistable chains, and men driven to the closest recesses, where prone to indolence and inactivity, they endeavour by forcing nature and promoting dissipation to alleviate the distresses of their situation, until the season of their deliverance shall arrive.

Thus favoured did we imagine ourselves, whilst ancient and modern history inclined to confirm our belief, that we had availed ourselves of our advantages. It remained for America to discover and proclaim that Englishmen on the contrary, were wanting in all those qualities for which they are esteemed in the world - Enemies to liberty, deficient in courage, void of humanity - In short, without genius, principle, resolution or affection.

How little did we know of our future masters, or of their abode! when we fancied that North America in point of climate and situation was as inferior to the rest of the habitable globe as Europe is superior (‡) and that the constitutions, genius and dispositions of the inhabitants were influenced by these circumstances! For it seemed to us, judging from general nature, as well as from its apparent effects upon the climate of North-America, that this continent being covered with damp and impervious woods which cannot possibly be cleared in any proportion for a thousand years to come, is now, and must for many ages continue to be deprived of the genial and purifying influence of the sun and air: that the lakes of fresh water to an immense extent on the North, in the heats of summer increase the stagnation, humidity and putrefaction of air, peculiar to every uncleared country, and in the winter operate like the ice cellar of nature upon this new world is adding to the severity of the frost,; so that the country, although seemingly laying in temperate latitudes, labours during summer under a heat equal to that of the torrid zone, and in the winter experiences a severity of weather unknown without the frozen zones: And thus against the common order of nature even when in her severest mood, the human frame is racked between the violence of those opposite extremes, which constant experience has proved to be equally prejudicial to the powers of the mind, to animal nature, and to all the other materials of which this globe is composed - for wood, stone and steel, fall to shatters from the sudden extremes of heat and cold: and the Negroes of Guinea do not pant under a hotter summer's sun, than the inhabitants of British America, nor have the people of Iceland their brains and blood more chill'd, or their limbs more bound by the winter's frost.

In other respects, North America did not appear to be favoured by nature in any other points that might alleviate her disadvantages. The little gu[s]ts from the sea that enter the land, instead of being large enough to furnish a sufficient quantity of air impregnated with salt to have a salubrious influence upon the general climate,|| too narrow even to counterballance the baneful effects of their swampy margins § - The whole coast of the United States, not exceeding in extent one half of the shores of the British Islands, and the land laying within any reasonable distance of the sea, almost without exception a barren land,¶ with a great proportion of it low and unwholsome to an extreme degree; whilst the tremendous Apalachian mountains at no great distance behind, running along the back of the provinces, leave but a narrow intermediate space of such land and climate as would be held to be habitable in Europe*.

Thus the mighty seat of western empire, so sublimely held forth to our future view by the prophets of America, appeared to us a stripe of scattered tracts in an inferior climate, so extended, broken and intersected, as never to be capable of any collected strength or steady union, and so extremely narrow as not to admit of the establishment of any principalities, commonwealths or other communities of sufficient strength for their own defence and security, much less of force to command independent respect among the powerful states of the earth - And it is with the utmost horror and contrition of mind that we confess that the British Colonies in the days of our ignorance appeared to us comparable to a lady, that, altho' neither of a very good constitution or disposition, was a *convenience to her keeper, who however little faith he might have in her gratitude or fidelity, had reason to trust that she being naturally helpless, and neither handsome or amiable, would scarce be weak enough to quit his protection and good offices, to become a common prostitute in the world, where those who might seduce her, after she had served their turn, would naturally leave her to her fate, when it would be too late to return to her old and steady friend JOHN BULL.*

‡ As a proof of the temperature of the climate of Europe it is inhabited ten degrees farther from the sun than any other quarter of the globe. Moreover every man who has observed the people of America and of Europe, will allow that Frenchmen, &c. of forty, are ten years younger in constitution than Americans of the same age, and as much older than Englishmen.

|| Cheseapeak, the only inlet that deserves a name, after mention of the Mediterranean, Baltic, or Black Seas, is not one hundredth part of their extent, and the water, except at the mouth, almost fresh.

§ Witness the unwholsomeness of the Lower Counties of Delaware, of the eastern shore of Maryland, of both shores of Virginia, of Albemarle Sound, & c. The inhabitants of all which endeavour in spite of nature to enjoy the advantages of a near navigation at the expence of their constitutions, and indeed at the hazard of their lives.

¶ Almost the whole sea coast of New-England extremely barren, and the shores to the southward both of the Jersies, Virginia and the Carolinas are not only barren but unwholesome to an extreme.

* With regard to the chimera of an empire to be established at the back of those mountains, south sea dreams are now out of date, and men, taught by the sad experience of their fathers, listen with calmness to the suggestions of reason and experience. Those who still require to be cured of that frenzy by the specific waters of the Mississippi, will do well to consider, that there is an instance

upon record of a country so totally excluded from commerce and intercourse with the rest of the world that ever reared a people. Even the fertile tract of land upon the Boristhenes to the south of the Ukrain, altho' already cleared, and near to countries that are over peopled, with the advantage too of a river that is to be navigated upwards as well as downwards, (whereas the Mississippi can only be ascended with canoes, and that with such immense labour and delays, that nothing of any bulk could possibly be brought up the stream) never has been, and in all human probability never will be settled and cultivated.[94]

Appendix E: Letter of Anthony Allaire about the Battle of Kings Mountain and its Aftermath

King's Mountain
Extract of a Letter from Lieutenant Anthony Allaire Adjutant for Ferguson's Corps in the Carolinas *The Royal Gazette, (New York), February 24, 1781*

Extract from a letter from an officer, dated Charlestown, January 30th, 1781.

This gentleman went from New York with a detachment drawn from the Provincial Brigade, which was commanded by the brave Major Patrick FERGUSON.

This letter gives the most circumstantial account yet received of the action at King's Mountain, in South Carolina, Oct. seventh.

"I think the last letter I wrote you was from Fort Moultrie, which I left a few days after.

We marched to a place called Ninety Six, which is about two hundred miles from Charleston; we lay there about a fortnight in good quarters, after which we proceeded to the frontiers of South Carolina, and frequently passed the line into North Carolina, and can say with propriety, that there is not a regiment or detachment of his Majesty's service, that ever went through the fatigues, or suffered so much, as our detachment.

That you may have some faint idea of our suffering, I shall mention a few particulars.

In the first place we were separated from all the army, acting with the militia; we never lay two nights in one place, frequently making forced marches of twenty and thirty miles in one night; skirmishing very often; the greatest part of our time without rum or wheat flour-rum is a very essential article, for in marching ten miles we would often be obliged to ford two or three rivers, which wet the men up to their waists.

In this disagreeable situation, we remained till the seventh of October, when we were attacked by two thousand five hundred Rebels, under the command of Gen. Williams.

Col. FERGUSON had under his command eight hundred militia, and our detachment, which at that time was reduced to an hundred men.

The action commenced about two o'clock in the afternoon, and was very severe for upwards of an hour, during which the Rebels were charged and drove back several times, with considerable slaughter.

When our detachment charged, for the first time, it fell to my lot to put a Rebel Captain to death, which I did most effectually, with one blow of my sword; the fellow was at least six feet high, but I had rather the advantage, as I was mounted on an elegant horse, and he on foot.

But their numbers enabled them to surround us and the North Carolina regiment, which consisted of about three hundred men.

Seeing this, and numbers being out of ammunition which naturally threw the rest of the militia into confusion, our gallant little detachment, which consisted of only seventy men, exclusive of twenty who acted as dragoons, and ten who drove wagons, etc., when we marched to the field of action, were all killed and wounded but twenty, and those brave fellows were soon crowded into an heap by the militia.

Capt. DePEYSTER, on whom the command devolved, seeing it impossible to form six men together, thought it necessary to surrender, to save the lives of the brave men who were left.

We lost in this action, Maj. FERGUSON, of the Seventy-first regiment, a man strongly attached to his King and country, well informed in the art of war, brave, humane, and an agreeable companion-in short, he was universally esteemed in the army, and I have every reason to regret his unhappy fate.

We lost eighteen men killed on the spot-Capt. RYERSON and thirty-two Sergeants and privates wounded, of Maj. FERGUSON's detachment.

Lieutenant M'GINNIS of ALLEN's regiment, Skinner's brigade, killed; taken prisoners, two Captains, four Lieutenants, three Ensigns, one Surgeon, and fifty-four Sergeants and privates, including the wounded, wagoners, etc.

The militia killed, one hundred, including officers; wounded, ninety; taken prisoners about six hundred; our baggage all taken, of course.

The Rebels lost Brig.-Gen. Williams, and one hundred and thirty-five, including officers, killed; wounded nearly equal to ours.

The morning after the action we were marched sixteen miles, previous to which orders were given by the Rebel Col. Campbell (whom the command devolved on) that should they be attacked on their march, they were to fire on, and destroy their prisoners.

The party was kept marching two days without any kind of provisions. The officers' baggage, on the third day's march, was all divided among the Rebel officers.

Shortly after we were marched to Bickerstaff's settlement, where we arrived on the thirteenth.

On the fourteenth, a court martial, composed of twelve field officers, was held for the trial of the militia prisoners; when, after a short hearing, they condemned thirty of the most principal and respectable characters, whom they considered to be most inimical to them, to be executed;

and, at six o'clock in the evening of the same day, executed Col. MILLS, Capt. CHITWOOD, Capt. WILSON, and six privates; obliging every one of their officers to attend at the death of those brave, but unfortunate Loyalists, who all, with their last breath and blood, held the Rebels and their cause as infamous and base, and as they were turning off, extolled their King and the British Government.

On the morning of the fifteenth, Col. Campbell had intelligence that Col. TARLETON was approaching him, when he gave orders to his men, that should Col. TARLETON come up with them, they were immediately to fire on Capt. DePEYSTER and his officers, who were in the front, and then a second volley on the men.

During this day's march the men were obliged to give thirty-five Continental dollars for a single ear of Indian corn, and forty for a drink of water, they not being allowed to drink when fording a river; in short, the whole of the Rebels' conduct from the surrender of the party into their hands is incredible to relate.

Several of the militia that were worn out with fatigue, and not being able to keep up, were cut down, and trodden to death in the mire.

After the party arrived at Moravian Town, in North Carolina, we officers were ordered in different houses. Dr. JOHNSON (who lived with me) and myself were turned out of our bed at an unseasonable hour of the night, and threatened with immediate death if we did not make room for some of Campbell's officers;

Dr. JOHNSON was, after this, knocked down, and treated in the basest manner, for endeavoring to dress a man whom they had cut on the march.

The Rebel officers would often go in amongst the prisoners, draw their swords, cut down and wound those whom their wicked and savage minds prompted.

This is a specimen of Rebel lenity-you may report it without the least equivocation, for upon the word and honor of a gentleman, this description is not equal to their barbarity. This kind of treatment made our time pass away very disagreeably.

After we were in Moravian Town about a fortnight, we were told we could not get paroles to return within the British lines; neither were we to have any till we were moved over the mountains in the back parts of Virginia, where we were to live on hoe cake and milk;

In consequence of this, Capt. TAYLOR, Lieut. STEVENSON and myself, chose rather to trust the hand of fate, and agreeable to our inclinations, set out from Moravian Town the fifth of November, and arrived at the British lines the twentieth.

From this town to Ninety Six, which was the first post we arrived at, is three hundred miles; and from Ninety Six to Charlestown, two hundred, so that my route was five hundred miles.

The fatigues of this jaunt I shall omit till I see you, although I suffered exceedingly; but thank God am now in Charlestown in good quarters." [95]

Appendix F: 1764 Manual of Arms

The Manual Exercise, as Ordered By His Majesty, in 1764.

I. Poise your Firelocks! *Two Motions.*

> ***1st.*** *Seize the Firelock with your right Hand, and turn the* Lock outwards,
>> *keeping the Firelock perpendicular.*
>
> ***2d.*** *Bring up the Firelock with a quick Motion from the* Shoulder, and
>> *seize it with the left Hand just above the Lock, so that the* little Finger may
>> *rest upon the Spring, and the Thumb lie upon the Stock ; The* Firelock
>> *must not be held too far from the Body, and the left Hand* must be of equal
>> *height with the Eyes.*

II. Cock your Firelocks! *Two Motions.*

> ***1st.*** *Turn the Barrel opposite to your Face, and place your* Thumb upon
>> *the Cock, raising the Elbow square at this Motion.*
>
> ***2d.*** *Cock your Firelock, by drawing your Elbow down,* placing your
>> *Thumb upon the Breech Pin, and the Fingers under the* guard.

III. Present! *One Motion.*

> *Step back about six Inches to the Rear with the right Foot,* *bringing the left Toe to the Front ; at the same Time the Butt* *End of the Fire-lock must be brought to an equal Height with* *your Shoulder, placing the left Hand on the Swell, and the* *Fore-Finger of the right Hand before the Tricker, (Trigger*)* *sinking the Muzzle a little.*

IV. Fire! *One Motion.*

Pull the Tricker (Trigger*) *briskly, and immediately after bringing up the right*

Foot, come to the Priming Position, with the Lock opposite to the right

Breast, the Muzzle the height of the Hat, keeping it firm and steady, and at

the same Time seize the Cock with the Fore-Finger and Thumb of the right

Hand, the back of the Hand turn'd up.

[To come to the Priming Position, bring the right Foot up and place the

right Heel behind the Left. The Body should be half-faced to the Right with

the Barrel pointing straight forward.]

V. Half Cock your Firelocks! *One Motion.*

Half bend the Cock briskly with a draw back of the right Elbow, bringing

it close to the Butt of the Firelock.

VI. Handle your Cartridge! *One Motion.*

Bring your right Hand with a short Round to your Pouch, slapping it

hard ; seize the Cartridge, an bring it with a quick Motion to your Mouth,

bite the Top well off and bring the Hand as low as the Chin, with the

Elbow down.

VII. Prime! *One Motion.*

Shake the Powder into the Pan, placing the three last Fingers behind the

Hammer, with the Elbow up.

VIII. Shut your Pans! *Two Motions.*

1st. Shut your Pan briskly, drawing your right Arm at this motion towards

your Body, holding the Cartridge fast in your right Hand, as in the former

Position.

2d. Turn the Piece nimbly round to the loading Position, with the Lock

to the Front, and the Muzzle the Height of the Chin, bringing the right

Hand behind the Muzzle ; both Feet kept fast in this Motion.

Recommended Web Resources

The links listed below were all valid at time of publication.
Molds:
Jeff Tanner Molds UK
http://www.jt-bullet-moulds.co.uk/

Ferguson parts:
The Rifle Shoppe
http://www.therifleshoppe.com

Books about gun building:
Track of the Wolf, Inc.
http://www.trackofthewolf.com

Flints, miscellaneous parts, tools:
Track of the Wolf, Inc.
http://www.trackofthewolf.com

Information about reenacting:
Hesse Kassel Jaeger Korps website
http://www.jaegerkorps.org

Information about Loyalists in the American Revolution
http://www.royalprovincial.com/index.htm

Information about gun building:
http://www.gunsmithy.com
http://www.americanlongrifles.com/index.htm

Honourable Company of Horners:
http://www.hornguild.org/

The Company of Military Historians:
 http://www.military-historians.org/

Contemporary Long Rifle Association:
http://www.longrifle.ws

American Long Rifle Association:
http://www.longrifle.org/

Miscellaneous Websites:

Online library of the Southern Campaign of the American
Revolution
http://jrshelby.com/sc-links/sc-texts.htm#btexts

A discussion of the Ferguson Rifle
http://web.archive.org/web/19990428111256/www.southdoc.net/tnc
hron/ferguson2.htm

Christie's Auction house A Rare 32-Bore French Breech-Loading
Flintlock Pistol On The La Chaumette System
http://www.christies.com/LotFinder/lot_details.aspx?pos=6&intObje
ctID=3103340&sid=

List of firearms from The Heritage Plantation collection
http://www.h-net.org/~ieahcweb/revtest/guns/gunindex.html

Dr Gilchrist's magnificent site on Patrick Ferguson
http://www.silverwhistle.co.uk/lobsters/ferguson.html

The Society of 18th Century Gentlemen: Shooting page
http://www.ballindalloch-press.com/society/shooting.html

Firearms, long range target shooting and associated history
http://www.researchpress.co.uk/

National Rifle Association
http://www.nra.org

National Muzzleloading Rifle Association
http://www.nmlra.org

Bibliography

The American Rifleman: NRA Publications: August & September 1971

Acton, John, An Essay on Shooting: **ISBN-13:** 978-1104022464 Richmond Publishing Co., Ltd., 1975

Blackmore, Howard L., Firearms: **ASIN:** B000Y86YTO Published 1964 by Studio Vista Limited

Blackmore, Howard L., Gunmakers of London Supplement 1350-1850: **ISBN-13:** 978-0888550132 Museum Restoration Service (1999)

Blackmore, Howard L., Gunmakers of London 1350-1850: **ISBN-13:** 978-0873870948 George Shumway Publisher (April 1986)

Blackmore, Howard L., Guns and Rifles of the World: **ISBN-13:** 978-0670357802 Studio; First edition (September 3, 1965)

Blackmore, Howard L., Hunting Weapons from the Middle Ages to the Twentieth Century: Dover Publications; **ISBN-13:** 978-0486409610 Dover Publications; Dover Ed edition (March 31, 2000)

Baker, Ezekiel, Twenty Three years Practice and Observation with Rifle Guns   **ISBN-13:** 978-1120047595 Kessinger Publishing, LLC (August 26, 2009)

Cornelison, John E., Jr., Victory and Retribution: An Archeological Survey at Kings Mountain National Military Park South Carolina SEAC Accession Number 1389

Canfield, Bruce N.; Lamoreaux, Robert L.; Johnson, Edward R.; Bailey, De Witt, British Military Flintlock Rifles, 1740-1840: **ISBN-13:** 978-1931464031 Andrew Mowbray Pub (August 1, 2002)

Collins, James, Autobiography of a Revolutionary Soldier: **ISBN** 0-405-11850-3 Ayer Company Publishers Inc. 1980

Diderot, Denis, Encyclopedia of Technology *Encyclopédie; ou, Dictionnaire raisonné des sciences, des arts, et des métiers.* Le Breton publisher *Paris* 1751

Dunkerly, Robert M., The Battle of Kings Mountain: Eyewitness Accounts **ISBN**-13: 978-1596292369 The History Press, March 20, 2007

Draper, Lyman C., Kings Mountain and its Heroes: **ISBN-13:** 978-1570720604 Overmountain Press; Second edition (January 1, 1996)

Ewald, Johann, Diary of the American War: A Hessian Journal ISBN 0-300-02153-4 Yale University Press; Second US edition (July 1, 1979)

Ferguson, James, Two Scottish Soldiers and a Jacobite Laird Aberdeen, D. Wyllie & Son 1888

Ferguson, Adam, BIOGRAPHICAL SKETCH, OR MEMOIR,OF LIEUTENANT-COLONEL PATRICK FERGUSON ORIGINALLY INTENDED FOR THE BRITISH ENCYCLOPEDIA EDINBURGH :PRINTED BY JOHN MOIR, ROYAL BANK CLOSE. 1817.

Hagist, Don N. ed., A British Soldier's Story, Roger Lamb's Narrative of the American Revolution: **ISBN** 9-893832-12-0 Baraboo, WI: Ballindalloch Press, 2004.

Held, Robert, The Age of Firearms: A Pictorial History: **ISBN-13:** 978-0517246665 Bonanza Publishing 1978

Gilchrist, M. M., Patrick Ferguson "A man of some genius" : **ISBN-13:** 978-1901663747 NMSE - Publishing Ltd (16 Jun 2003)

Hopkins, Alfred F., "Testing the Ferguson Rifle: Modern Marksman Attains High Precision With Arm of 1776[*]" Dr. Alfred F. Hopkins, formerly Field Curator, Museum Division, Washington. The Regional Review, National Park Service, Region One, Richmond, Va., Vol. VI, Nos. 1 and 2.

Instructions for Loading & Cleaning the Whitworth Patent Military Rifle 1860

"Ferguson's Breechloading Rifles" The Gun Report November 1963.

Klein, Lance, "This Barbarous Weapon" Muzzle Blasts 2000

Layton Hillyer, "Ferguson—A Man and his Rifle" Guns and Ammo June 1960

McGuire, Thomas J., Battle of Paoli ISBN 978-0-8117-3337-3 Stackpole Books July 2000

Moss, Bobby Gilmer. Ed., Uzal Johnson, Loyalist Surgeon: A Revolutionary War Diary ISBN-13: 978-0962617270 Scotia Hibernia Press (2000)

Moss, Bobby Gilmer, ed., Journal of Capt. Alexander Chesney: Adjutant to Major Patrick Ferguson ISBN-13: 978-0962617287 Scotia-Hibernia Press (2002)

Mowday, Bruce E., September 11, 1777 Washington's Defeat at Brandywine Dooms Philadelphia ISBN-13: 978-1572493285 White Mane Publishing Company; First edition (December 2002)

Newman George C., Swords and Blades of the American Revolution : ISBN-13: 978-1880655009 Scurlock Publishing Company (February 1, 1995)

Newman George C., Battle Weapons of the American Revolution: ISBN-13: 978-1880655078 Scurlock Pub Co (January 1998)

Newman George C.; Kravic, Frank, Collector's Illustrated Encyclopedia of the American Revolution: **ISBN-13:** 978-0811703949 Scurlock Publishing Company (January 1, 1990)

Royal Warrants 1764 Manual of Arms

Russell, C. P., "The American Rifle: At the Battle of Kings Mountain" C. P. Russell, Supervisor of Interpretation, Washington The Regional Review, National Park Service, Region One, Richmond, Va., Vol. V, No. 1, July 1940, pp. 15-21

Sharp, Benjamin, Battle of King's Mountain Reuben T. Durrett Collection on Kentucky and the Ohio River Valley (University of Chicago. Library), University of Chicago. Library 1843

Shumway, George, Jaeger Rifles: **ASIN:** B0024HWXV6

Scythmore-Wedderburn papers: The National Archives of Scotland, H.M. General Register House, 2 Princes Street, Edinburgh, EH1 3YY
George Shumway
Tarassuk, Leonid; Blair, Claude, The Complete Encyclopedia of Arms & Weapons: **ISBN-13:** 978-0671422578 Simon & Schuster Publishing (November 30, 1982)

Young, Rogers W., "Kings Mountain, A Hunting Rifle Victory" Rogers W. Young, Assistant Historical Technician, Branch of Historic Sites The Regional Review, National Park Service, Region One, Richmond, Va., Vol. III, No. 6, December 1939, pp. 25-29

Endnotes

[1] Gilchrist, M. M., Patrick Ferguson "A man of some genius" : NMS Publishing Ltd (16 Jun 2003)... Pg 3

[2] Ibid... Pg 3

[3] Scythmore-Wedderburn papers: The National Archives of Scotland, H.M. General Register House, 2 Princes Street, Edinburgh, EH1 3YY...783, 140/2/57

[4] Gilchrist, M. M., Patrick Ferguson "A man of some genius": NMS Publishing Ltd (16 Jun 2003)...Pg 8 & 9

[5] Klein, Lance. This Barbarous Weapon" Muzzle Blasts 2000

[6] Scythmore-Wedderburn papers: The National Archives of Scotland, H.M. General Register House, 2 Princes Street, Edinburgh, EH1 3YY ...783, 140/2/36

[7] Scythmore-Wedderburn papers: The National Archives of Scotland, H.M. General Register House, 2 Princes Street, Edinburgh, EH1 3YY...783, 140/2/44

[8] Gilchrist, M. M., Patrick Ferguson "A man of some genius" : NMS Publishing Ltd (16 Jun 2003)...Pg 23

[9] Gilchrist, M. M., Patrick Ferguson "A man of some genius": NMS Publishing Ltd (16 Jun 2003)....Pg 24 & 25

[10] ibid ...Pg 24 & 25

[11] Klein, Lance. This Barbarous Weapon" Muzzle Blasts 2000

[12] Gilchrist, M. M., Patrick Ferguson "A man of some genius": NMS Publishing Ltd (16 Jun 2003)...Pg 24 & 25

[13] Ibid...Pg 28

[14] Ibid... Pg 28

[15] Scythmore-Wedderburn papers: The National Archives of Scotland, H.M. General Register House, 2 Princes Street, Edinburgh, EH1 3YY...783, 140/2/50

[16] Scythmore-Wedderburn papers: The National Archives of Scotland, H.M. General Register House, 2 Princes Street, Edinburgh, EH1 3YY ...783, 140/2/64-65

[17] Gilchrist, M. M. Patrick Ferguson "A man of some genius" ...Pg 33

[18] Acton, John, An Essay on Shooting: Richmond Publishing Co., Ltd., 1975

[19] Scythmore-Wedderburn papers: The National Archives of Scotland, H.M. General Register House, 2 Princes Street, Edinburgh, EH1 3YY...783,140/2/57

[20] Scythmore-Wedderburn papers: The National Archives of Scotland, H.M. General Register House, 2 Princes Street, Edinburgh, EH1 3YY...783,140/2/48

[21] Scythmore-Wedderburn papers: The National Archives of Scotland, H.M. General Register House, 2 Princes Street, Edinburgh, EH1 3YY ...783,140/1/43

[22] Scythmore-Wedderburn papers: The National Archives of Scotland, H.M. General Register House, 2 Princes Street, Edinburgh, EH1 3YY ...783,140/1/43

[23] Scythmore-Wedderburn papers: The National Archives of Scotland, H.M. General Register House, 2 Princes Street, Edinburgh, EH1 3YY ...783,140/1/43

[24] Baker, Ezekiel, Twenty Three years Practice and Observation with Rifle Guns Kessinger Publishing, LLC (August 26, 2009) ...Plates 1-4

[25] Canfield, Bruce N.; Lamoreaux, Robert L.; Johnson, Edward R.; Bailey, De Witt, British Military Flintlock Rifles, 1740-1840: Andrew Mowbray Pub (August 1, 2002) Pg 44

[26] Ibid...Pg 44-45

[27] Scythmore-Wedderburn papers: The National Archives of Scotland, H.M. General Register House, 2 Princes Street, Edinburgh, EH1 3YY ...783, 140/2/70-71

[28] Edinburgh University Library, Laing MSS,...La 11, 456

[29] Edinburgh University Library, Laing MSS ...La 11, 456

[30] Edinburgh University Library, Laing MSS...La 11, 456

[31] Canfield, Bruce N.; Lamoreaux, Robert L.; Johnson, Edward R.; Bailey, De Witt, British Military Flintlock Rifles, 1740-1840: Andrew Mowbray Pub (August 1, 2002) ...Pg 51

[32] Ibid...Pg 52

[33] Ibid...Pg 52

[34] Ibid...Pg 54

[35] Ibid...Pg 55

[36] Gilchrist, M. M., Patrick Ferguson "A man of some genius": NMS Publishing Ltd (16 Jun 2003)...Pg 75

[37] Scythmore-Wedderburn papers: The National Archives of Scotland, H.M. General Register House, 2 Princes Street, Edinburgh, EH1 3YY...783, 140/2/89

[38] Scythmore-Wedderburn papers: The National Archives of Scotland, H.M. General Register House, 2 Princes Street, Edinburgh, EH1 3YY...783,140/2/89

[39] Gilchrist, M. M. Patrick Ferguson "A man of some genius" ... Pg 46

[40] Ibid...Pg 46 & 47

[41] Ibid...Pg 47

[42] Ibid...Pg 52

[43] Ferguson, James, Two Scottish Soldiers and a Jacobite Laird Aberdeen, D. Wyllie & Son 1888...Pg 80

[44] Scythmore-Wedderburn papers: The National Archives of Scotland, H.M. General Register House, 2 Princes Street, Edinburgh, EH1 3YY...783,140/2/85

[45] University of Michigan, William L. Clements Library, Sir Henry Clinton Papers, Volume 80, item 8

[46] Acadiensis Vol. 6, No. 4, October 1906

[47] Acadiensis Vol. 6, No. 4, October 1906

[48] Ferguson, James, Two Scottish Soldiers and a Jacobite Laird Aberdeen, D. Wyllie & Son 1888...Page 80-81

[49] Gilchrist, M. M., Patrick Ferguson "A man of some genius" : NMS Publishing Ltd (16 Jun 2003) ...Pg 61

[50] Ibid...Pg 61

[51] Canfield, Bruce N.; Lamoreaux, Robert L.; Johnson, Edward R.; Bailey, De Witt, British Military Flintlock Rifles, 1740-1840: Andrew Mowbray Pub (August 1, 2002)...Pg 215

[52] Gilchrist, M. M., Patrick Ferguson "A man of some genius": NMS Publishing Ltd (16 Jun 2003)...Pg 65

53   Ibid …Pg 65
54   Ewald, Johann, Diary of the American War: A Hessian Journal Yale
University Press; Second US edition (July 1, 1979)… Pg 242
55   Ferguson, James, Two Scottish Soldiers and a Jacobite Laird
Aberdeen, D. Wyllie & Son 1888… Pg 83
56   Sharp, Benjamin, Battle of King's Mountain Reuben T. Durrett
Collection on Kentucky and the Ohio River Valley University of Chicago. Library
1843…Pg 46-47
57   "A letter from a Royalist officer" attributed to Allaire Published
Charlestown, January 30th, 1781, and published in Rivington's Royal Gazette,
New York, February 24, 1781
       (Published in the Virginia Gazette, November 11, 1780;, Draper's King's
       Mountain and Its Heroes, 204)
59   Pension application Aaron Deveny Jr 25 November 1834
60   Pension application Aaron Deveny Jr 25 November 1834
61   Pension application Aaron Deveny Jr 25 November 1834
62   Gilchrist, M. M., Patrick Ferguson "A man of some genius": NMS
Publishing Ltd (16 Jun 2003)…Pg 67
63   Ibid…Pg 67
64   Ferguson, James, Two Scottish Soldiers and a Jacobite Laird
Aberdeen, D. Wyllie & Son 1888…Pg 92
65   Cornelison, John E., Jr., Victory and Retribution: An Archeological
Survey at Kings Mountain National Military Park South Carolina SEAC
Accession Number 1389…Pg 34
66   Ferguson, James, Two Scottish Soldiers and a Jacobite Laird
Aberdeen, D. Wyllie & Son 1888…Pg 100
67   Canfield, Bruce N.; Lamoreaux, Robert L.; Johnson, Edward R.; Bailey,
De Witt, British Military Flintlock Rifles, 1740-1840: Andrew Mowbray Pub
(August 1, 2002) Pg 215
68   Collins, James, Autobiography of a Revolutionary Soldier: Ayer
Company Publishers Inc. 1980
69   Canfield, Bruce N.; Lamoreaux, Robert L.; Johnson, Edward R.; Bailey,
De Witt, British Military Flintlock Rifles, 1740-1840: Andrew Mowbray Pub
(August 1, 2002) Pg 214
70   Ibid… Pg 215
71   Instructions Whitworth Rifle
72   Canfield, Bruce N.; Lamoreaux, Robert L.; Johnson, Edward R.; Bailey,
De Witt, British Military Flintlock Rifles, 1740-1840: Andrew Mowbray Pub
(August 1, 2002) Pg 41
73   Ibid… Pg 41
74   Baker, Ezekiel, Twenty Three years Practice and Observation with Rifle
Guns Kessinger Publishing, LLC (August 26, 2009) … Pg 72

[75]   Canfield, Bruce N.; Lamoreaux, Robert L.; Johnson, Edward R.; Bailey, De Witt, British Military Flintlock Rifles, 1740-1840:   Andrew Mowbray Pub (August 1, 2002)   Pg 11
[76]   ibid

         Pg 11
[77]   Klein, Lance. This Barbarous Weapon" Muzzle Blasts 2000
[78]   American Rifleman Magazine   1971
[79]   Blackmore, Howard L., Firearms: Published 1964 by Studio Vista Limited
[80]   Blackmore, Howard L., Gunmakers of London Supplement 1350-1850: Museum Restoration Service (1999)
[81]   Blackmore, Howard L., Gunmakers of London Supplement 1350-1850: Museum Restoration Service (1999)
[82]   Canfield, Bruce N.; Lamoreaux, Robert L.; Johnson, Edward R.; Bailey, De Witt, British Military Flintlock Rifles, 1740-1840:   Andrew Mowbray Pub (August 1, 2002)   Pg 19
[83]   Ibid...Pg 24
[84]   Ibid...Pg 26
[85]   Ibid...Pg 26
[86]   Scythmore-Wedderburn papers: The National Archives of Scotland, H.M. General Register House, 2 Princes Street, Edinburgh, EH1 3YY...783, 140/2/89
[87]   Scythmore-Wedderburn papers: The National Archives of Scotland, H.M. General Register House, 2 Princes Street, Edinburgh, EH1 3YY...783, 140/2/86
[88]   Scythmore-Wedderburn papers: The National Archives of Scotland, H.M. General Register House, 2 Princes Street, Edinburgh, EH1 3YY...783, 140/2/87
         Scrymgeour-Wedderburn Papers, NRA(S) 783, 140/2/78, originally enclosed in 140/2/77
[90]   Scythmore-Wedderburn papers: The National Archives of Scotland, H.M. General Register House, 2 Princes Street, Edinburgh, EH1 3YY...783, 140/2/79
[91]   Scythmore-Wedderburn papers: The National Archives of Scotland, H.M. General Register House, 2 Princes Street, Edinburgh, EH1 3YY 783, 140/1/187, originally enclosed in 140/2/79
[92] Scythmore-Wedderburn papers: The National Archives of Scotland, H.M. General Register House, 2 Princes Street, Edinburgh, EH1 3YY 783, 140/1/188, originally in 783, 140/2/79
[93]   Scythmore-Wedderburn papers: The National Archives of Scotland, H.M. General Register House, 2 Princes Street, Edinburgh, EH1 3YY 783, 140/1/189, originally enclosed in 783, 140/2/79
[94]   Scythmore-Wedderburn papers: The National Archives of Scotland, H.M. General Register House, 2 Princes Street, Edinburgh, EH1 3YY 783, 140/1/186, originally enclosed in 140/2/79, and 140/1/190 (less legible copy), formerly enclosed with 783, 140/2/80
[95]   The Royal Gazette, (New York), February 24, 1781

Index

General Von Knyphausen, 60
Governor General of Quebec, 29
Granada, 33
grave, 25, 28, 29, 172
groves, 104
gun makers, 35, 148, 160
Half Cock, 113, 211
hang their leaders, 85
Henry Clinton, 74, 187
Henry VIII, 145, 151
Hessian Jaeger, 145
Hirst, 32, 160
Howard Blackmore, 13, 215
Howe, 34, 49, 57, 70, 187
Hume, 85, 172
Husbands, 92
Hussar, 63, 67
in Chief of the Royal Regiment of Artillery, 37
Jacobite, 25
Jaeger, 13, 16, 17, 95, 143, 145, 163, 164, 166, 167, 213, 218
Jäger, 20, *See* Jaeger
James Collins, 92, 96, 216
James Ferguson, 25
John Acton, 44, 215
July 1778, 62
King George III, 120, 131
King's Bounty, 58
Kings Mountain, 16, 27, 29, 56, 70, 84, 85, 90, 91, 92, 93, 95, 96, 97, 99, 102, 136, 173, 205, 215, 216, 218
Kit Ravenshear, 13
La Petite Guerre, 34, 72
lands, 71, 104, 137
Light Infantry, 27, 34, 69, 70, 72, 93, 95, 107, 109, 142
Living Historians, 15
Living History Interpreters, 15
Loading and Firing, 111
lock, 16, 24, 123, 126, 132, 134, 145, 162, 164, 210
London, 29, 39, 47, 57, 148, 155, 215
Long land pattern muskets, 148
Long rifles, 111, 166
Lord Barington, 33
Lord Cathcart, 145
Lord Elibank, 25
Lord townsend, 45
Louisborg, 145
Loyal American Volunteers, 74, 91
Loyal Americans Volunteers Company, 95
Loyalist, 57, 71, 82, 91, 92, 93, 94, 95, 145
Lubing the Breech, 116
lubricant, 116, 127
M. M. Gilchrist, 14
Major Timpany, 90
manual of arms 1764, 149
Master general of Ordnance, 37, 45
militia, 56, 57, 62, 74, 82, 90, 94, 95, 165, 166, 176, 187, 188, 206, 207, 208
Milwaukee Public Museum, 32, 135
morse taper, 41
Musket, 18, 38, 67, 115, 160
Muzzle loaders, 21
Narragansett, 15, 105, 129

Author Biographies

Ricky Roberts and Bryan Brown are two historical reenactors and amateur historians with a bit of a bug for the firelocks and an itch for Patrick Ferguson's Breech loading Ordnance Rifle, specifically. In an era when most other arms loaded from the muzzle and smoothbore arms were in the vast majority Patrick Ferguson developed what is in our opinion the ultimate pre-cartridge firearm, certainly the coolest flintlock era weapon.

Ricky is no novice; he has been reenacting and shooting black powder since the 1970s and is a former member of the US International Muzzle Loading team. He has represented the US at many international competitions shooting anything from a matchlock, through a caplock both in long arms and pistols. He is a member of the New Acquisition Militia, The Widowmakers, Hesse Kassel Jaeger Korps, American Long Rifle Association, The National Muzzle Loading Rifle Association, and National Rifle Association, a regular attendee of the NMLRA Friendship National

Championship shoots and is a retired US Postal Worker. Ricky is the author of "The Ramblings of a Shirttailed Man" which runs occasionally in On the Trail magazine

At one point in his research Ricky got pointed to Bryan Brown when they were on opposite sides at the Battle of Huck's Defeat at Brattonsville South Carolina. Ricky portrays a Rebel/Patriot Rifleman with the New Acquisition Militia, and Bryan is a founding member of the Hesse Kassel Jaeger Korps, a Crown/British forces Rifle unit brought over to hunt American Riflemen. They had been shooting at each other for years but they had not crossed paths socially as of yet.

Bryan has been a reenactor since 1977, having reenacted a variety of periods both in the US and in Europe. Prior to helping found the Hesse Kassel Jaeger Korps in 1995, he spent 6 years with the 71st Regiment of Highland Foote out of Maryland where he first began seriously digging into Ferguson and his rifle. Bryan is an armourer and gunsmith, having built and taught others to build hundreds of black powder arms and other hand-held weapons since the early

1980s. He "has something of a penchant for building oddball arms" and has a decent library of historical arms related resources. He has published books and articles on a variety of subjects, period and otherwise, and he is a member of The National Muzzle Loading Rifle Association, the National Rifle Association, the Honorable Company of Horners, the American Long Rifles, the Company of Military Historians, and various less formal groups of period gunsmiths and armourers. He is also a regular attendee of Chuck Dixon's annual Custom Muzzle Loading Faire, held in Kempton Pennsylvania. Bryan works for IBM when he isn't reenacting.

*Nock Volley Gun on loan from Steve Doyle, also known as"McJaeger,"

CPSIA information can be obtained at www.ICGtesting.com
Printed in the USA
LVOW071121310312

275587LV00008B/194/P